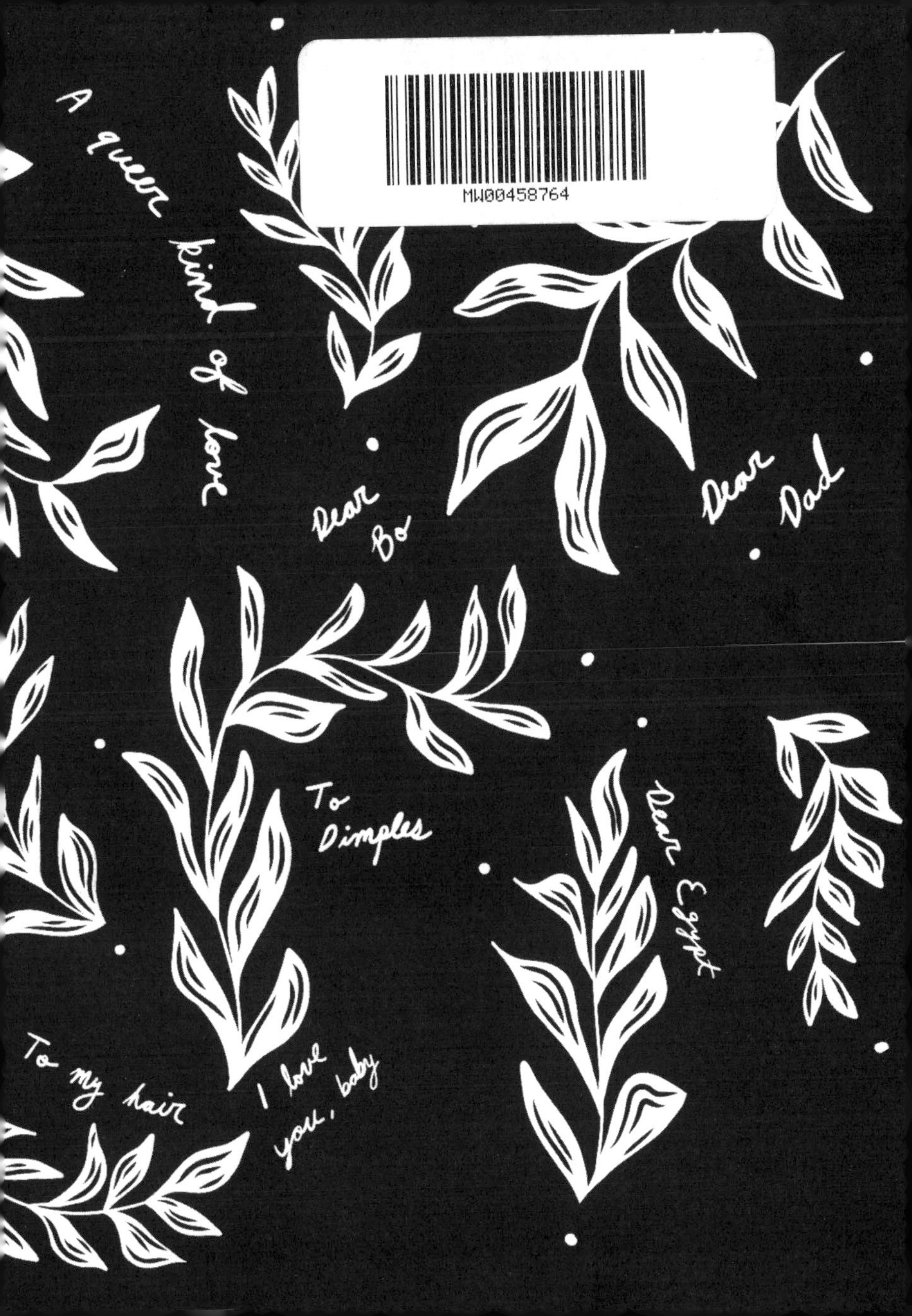
A queer kind of love
Dear Bo
Dear Dad
To Dimples
Dear Egypt
To my hair
I love you, baby

BLACK
LOVE
LETTERS

ART BY

NATALIE JOHNSON

BLACK LOVE LETTERS

EDITED BY COLE BROWN
AND NATALIE JOHNSON

GET LIFTED BOOKS

A zando IMPRINT

NEW YORK

GET LIFTED BOOKS

Get Lifted Books is an imprint of Zando.
zandoprojects.com

First Edition: October 2023

Text design by Aubrey Khan, Neuwirth & Associates, Inc.
Cover design by Alicia Tatone
Cover art by Natalie Johnson

The publisher does not have control over and is not responsible for author or other third-party websites (or their content).

Library of Congress Control Number: 2023933806

978-1-63893-120-1 (Hardcover)
978-1-63893-121-8 (ebook)

10 9 8 7 6 5 4 3 2 1
Manufactured in the United States of America

TO ALL OF US,
AND TO EVERY OUNCE
OF OUR LIVES THAT IS
DESERVING OF LOVE

CONTENTS

⦀ CARE

AWE

LOSS

IV AMBIVALENCE

V TRANSFORMATION

FOREWORD

BY JOHN LEGEND

DEAR CHRISSY,

I don't love you like I used to. When you first saw those words on the track list for my latest album, you raised an eyebrow. Why would I write a breakup song at this stage in our relationship? Was there something I needed to say? Well, of course, there was something I needed to say. I needed to tell you how proud I am of how we've grown together, how we've challenged and taught each other, how our love has evolved into something we never could have imagined when we first met. I don't love you like I used to.

I clearly recall the day you walked into my video set and lit up the room with your beauty, your infectious laugh, your wicked sense of humor. I instantly wanted to know you more. I wanted to approach your flame, hopeful that you would ignite something new in my life.

We think that men must teach boys to be men. That's how it worked in my life. My dad taught me how to take my time, to be a man of honor and character, to be a gentleman, to be a romantic. He showed me that love was how you spent your days, that time was a gift more precious than gold.

But some lessons I needed a woman to show me. I had folks to learn from for a time: my mother and grandmother. They fed my musical passions, showed me gospel piano, nurtured me in the church choir, and gave me an early love of learning. Then Grandma passed, and Mom began to struggle. She left, and for a long time—my growing years—my world lacked something crucial. I didn't know what I didn't know.

When you came along, my education began anew.

We met in a season in my life when I thought I'd made it. Some meet their loves early in life and fall at first sight. Not us; we took our time, exchanging texts and flirting from a distance for months before giving what we had a label. It happened when it had to. Any earlier, and I wouldn't have been ready. Any later, and I may have been too far along to stop and listen.

Where to start on all you've taught me? How to *really* cook. How to tell a (halfway decent) joke. The names of the Real Housewives. How to clean up after myself (some lessons, we're still working on). The two most powerful phrases in the English language: *I'm sorry* and *you're right*. Humility, humor, bravery, resilience, and vulnerability.

You've given me purpose. All I do, I do to support you and our growing family. It's granted my work, and my life, new meaning.

Watching you grow and nurture our babies is watching the wonder of creation itself. It's the closest I'll ever get to God. From the first breaths they took, I saw in them the best in you. Luna, with your smile, your sense of humor, and your meticulous attention to detail, and Miles, with your sense of adventure and intense zest for life.

As I write this, you're pregnant again. By the time the world sees this message, we will have welcomed a new little one into our lives.

Childbirth is beautiful and wondrous; it gave us two living miracles. Childbirth is also fragile, with the specter of violence and loss always hovering. We've experienced the soaring heights of its joys and the depths of its tragic possibilities.

After Luna was born, you slipped into a funk that stretched on for months before we knew what to call it: postpartum depression. The Chrissy that you and I both love vanished for a time. You struggled to leave the house, to even leave the couch, and your radiant smile shone less and less.

I didn't understand the condition then—neither of us did—so I tiptoed around the house fearing that I had done something to make you feel this way. That I had been responsible for dimming your light. When our doctor explained what you were experiencing, it was so relieving to know that this thing you were feeling was real. It had a name, and we could finally work to get you better.

Two years later, we already had two beautiful babies in our home when we were blessed with a third. Jack was a special kind of miracle—a natural pregnancy after years of struggling to conceive. Tragically, we never got the opportunity to share our love with him. We did all we could to support the life growing inside you; the doctors did all they could, but it wasn't enough. We couldn't stop the bleeding. Jack showed us that life is as precious as it is persistent. And sometimes, all the love in the world can't secure its survival.

We held Jack as long as we could before it was time to say goodbye. And then we mourned him together. If our love for Jack was massive, so was the grief he left behind. With time, the grief got easier to bear. It never disappeared, but it grew manageable. Jack was a part of you in a way he wasn't for me. You carried him inside you through twenty trying weeks. Still, sooner than I ever thought possible, you were ready to dream of growing our family again. Despite all your body, mind, and spirit had been through, you wanted to give it another shot.

I don't love you like I used to because my infatuation with you, my instant attraction to you, have evolved into something much more powerful—something forged by trials and fortified with a deep knowledge of each other and a commitment to building a household filled with love. You've shown me the power of resilience. If ever I am strong for you, it's because I've witnessed the strength you already have inside yourself. I marvel at your bravery, the way you've withstood existential challenges and come out the other side still joyful, still silly, still bighearted and emotionally generous. Like life, your spirit is persistent.

All of me loves all of you,
Your husband

MY POSTSCRIPT IS TO YOU, DEAR READER.

I have been in the entertainment business for a couple of decades now and have evolved, experimented, and expanded as a creator. I introduced myself to you with a piano and a microphone, but my curiosity led me in every direction—music, theater, film, television, philanthropy, entrepreneurship. Even as I widened my repertoire, one thing remained constant. If I look at my full body of work—the long list of projects I've touched from *Get Lifted* to *La La Land* to "All of Me"—the through line is love.

Love is the core of my art because it is the core of my life. I've loved and been loved in so many ways. I've felt the ecstasy of romance and the agony of loss and recognized love in both. It's the deepest emotion we human beings have, which is why it is an endless source of inspiration for me.

And there's something particularly special about Black Love.

When you consider the history of our people, the strife and adversity we've experienced and overcome, love seems an almost illogically ambitious act of resistance. We take pain and hardship and convert it into something that sustains us. We smile despite circumstance. We have the audacity to create ebullient, unapologetic art despite the world often telling us our lives don't matter. What could be braver?

There's no shortage of bad news today. Everywhere we look, there is division and suffering. Love is its salve. And art, at its best, injects that love into a world of hurt.

Which is why I just love this collection.

When Cole approached me with the idea of turning Natalie's beautiful letter series into a book, I knew I needed to support their work. They were kindred spirits, similarly driven to inject love into a difficult world. We set up Get Lifted Books with the mission of shining a light on brilliant creators like them who have stories to tell. I feel honored that they trusted us to bring their beautiful creation to life and grateful to have been asked to add my own entry, a letter to my wonderful wife.

So many people helped me get to where I am today. After two decades in this industry, I've reached a stage where all I do is in hopes of sending the ladder back down for the next generation. Cole and Natalie, as well as the many other creators in these pages, are voices worth hearing. Their pieces reflect the full range of human emotion: joy, grief, lust, hurt, and above all, love. Taken together, they've inspired me. They've reminded me of why I do what I do.

There are many books about love—love stories are some of our species' oldest—but precious few *are* love. That's a more difficult challenge—concentrating love to words on a page, capturing love as it is, delivering it still intact. Cole, Natalie, and the many authors in these pages have done just that—distilled love to soothe your soul.

I just know you'll love it like I do.

Best,
John

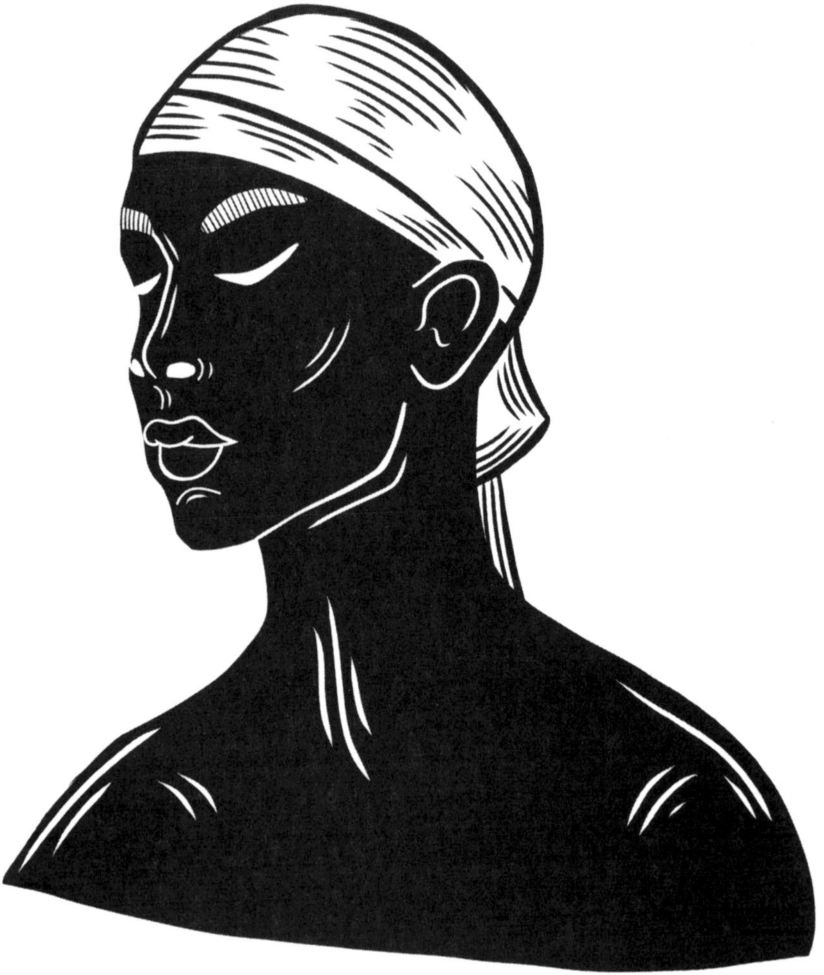

INTRODUCTION

When Darnella Frazier paused on the corner of 38th and Chicago Ave., she witnessed a white police officer violently rob a Black man of his life. The images of former Minneapolis police officer Derek Chauvin with his knee on George Floyd's neck are burned into the conscience of a generation.

At seventeen years old, Darnella became a national hero. Her presence of mind to capture those nine minutes and twenty-six seconds produced the definitive evidence that put that same officer behind bars. Without her video, the world would have known nothing more than what was concealed in a benign police report saying, "Man dies after medical incident during police interaction," and Derek Chauvin would have, literally, gotten away with murder.

But watching those minutes cost her. "A part of my childhood was taken from me," she wrote on the one-year anniversary of George Floyd's death.

The violence undoubtedly cost us too. The sight of Black death on repeat across social media and the news left many traumatized and weary. "Everyone I know is just so tired," Jenna Wortham wrote in the aftermath of twenty-year-old Daunte

Wright's killing in Brooklyn Center, Minnesota, mere miles from the Derek Chauvin trial underway.

Nothing explained the ubiquity of that trauma more than Darnella's testimony during the Chauvin trial: "When I look at George Floyd, I look at my dad. I look at my brothers. I look at my cousins, my uncles because they are all Black," she told the jury while fighting back the tears. "I look at that [video], and I look at how that could have been one of them."

We did too. We were among the weary. Like so many others, we listened to the constant drumbeat of Black death from the shut-in rooms of COVID lockdown—Natalie, in New York; Cole, in Sydney, Australia. We scrolled our timelines, watched and shared videos of the robbery, prayed that *this* precious life lost would be the last, and clenched fists in the face of our continued disappointment. We stayed attuned to the violence in hopes of saving each other and, in some ways, ourselves.

Black Love Letters was born in that moment in Natalie's heart and of Natalie's grief. She sought collective healing, a site for our people to come together on the deepest, strongest emotion we share. A place to exhibit the side of ourselves that wasn't so tainted by pain. A way to replenish the soul. She reached out to her creative friends and asked that they send love letters to the people, places, and things that meant the most to them—a small request born of big feelings.

Cole was one of the first people she called. We were longtime friends and short-time collaborators then, after coming together to work on Cole's first book. The project had the desired effect for us personally. It gave us a place to set our minds beyond the reach of tragedy.

We stumbled upon something subtle and profound: communal pain provides the possibility for shared deliverance—the possibility to carve out a space for healing, together. A possibility powered by Black Love, which has powers both awesome and unique; it invites the soul forward and nourishes it. In a country that so often tries to degrade us, to use us for its labor, to harm us, Black Love has always responded with force.

As early as the seventeenth century, enslaved Africans forged queer bonds on slave ships traveling between West Africa and the Caribbean, resisting the commodification of their stolen bodies. Omise'eke Natasha Tinsley, a scholar of the Black diaspora, writes that it is through this history that the Creole word "mati" finds its meaning: "figuratively mi mati is 'my girl,' but literally it means mate, as in shipmate—she who survived the Middle Passage with me."

From those earliest examples to today, Black Love has always been defined by its devotion, care, and intimacy but also its resistance, its unwavering ability to persist in a world that would rather quash it.

It is for this reason that we have gathered this collection of Black Love stories. We reserve this space for our humanity in all of its fond, ironic, elated, grief-stricken, confused glory. In the following pages you will find letters crafted by activists, statesmen, acclaimed and upcoming writers, artists, poets, and creators—all reflecting on what it means to be Black, to love, and to *be* loved in America.

Treat it like a stack of ribbon-tied letters on your doorstep. Read it in any order. Base it on what you need today. Dog-ear it. Sticky-note it. Come home to it. Return to it again and again and again when you need a little understanding. Write your own and pass it on. When you find yourself alone and downtrodden, when the news is too much, return to these pages.

This one is for you.

—Natalie and Cole

III

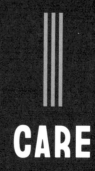

CARE

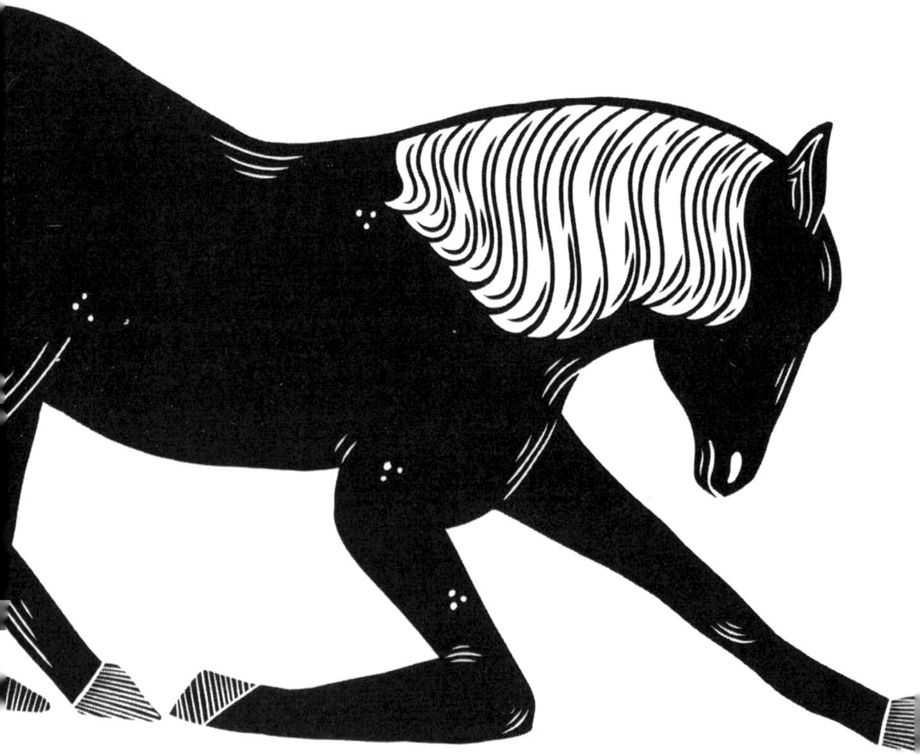

FOR JOYCETTA

BY JAMILA WOODS

This is a letter for you, Gramma J, published in a book you may or may not ever read, seeing as it's not the Bible. I can hear your voice in my head saying, "When will this child write something about herself for a change? Quit putting my name in alla this stuff..." I can see the hint of a smile on your face as you say it too—the smile that makes me think you secretly like being the sun in my universe, even if our orbits don't intersect as often as you'd like.

everything my grandma says is a poem. she is the topline writer, and i am the singer with no stories of her own. every story i own is a hand-me-down. except the ones about my uber drivers, i suppose.
i paid for those.

Here's your story as I remember it: When you were a little girl, you lived in Wabbaseka, Arkansas. You were the youngest of seven children.

3

You picked cotton in the fields with your oldest brother, James. You picked two hundred pounds of cotton a day. There was no electricity, no running water to make a bath. In the summer, you filled a tub of water from the well and waited for it to get hot. In the winter, you collected rainwater and heated it in a pot on the stove. Your parents were strict; they had to be. There were no telephones, but you could hear your mother calling you from five miles away.

> *in my worst dreams, Grandma splinters, says i never visit,*
> *says i quit Lasalle street, gave up grilled cheese on wonder bread,*
> *dropped out of sunday school, forgot dishes in the sink, flew off.*

I know, I know, I'm always leaving for somewhere, traveling home from someplace. I know it's too much to keep track of. I'm ashamed that I write metaphors about you more often than I call. When I do visit, I wonder if you can tell I'm trying to remember everything you say and do, taking voice memos, recording videos of you cooking recipes you never wrote down. I'm stocking up on memories in fear I won't have enough time to unlock them all. I'm embarrassed of the ways I've started to grieve you before you're even gone.

> *poetry is all about economy, fit. Grandma has a shortcut grace*
> *for when she's hungry: Jesus wept. Grandma never wastes anything.*

her pantry is full of exactly enough. in quarantine
i call to ask if i can order her anything. she says:
"if i don't have it, i don't need it."

My cousins and I beg you to take us on a trip to Wabbaseka.
You insist there's nothing there. The house is gone. You wouldn't
know the people. It's too hot. You say, "You crazier than a bessie
bug . . ." Joycetta, queen of idioms most people have never heard.
When I research your words, I find out that a bess beetle is a
cousin of the scarab beetle, native to Arkansas. They live inside
rotten logs and slowly eat them from the inside out. They live in
adult pairs with their dozens of kids, often taking care of their
offspring even after they grow into adults. Apparently, this
two-parent household lifestyle is rare for insects. Unusual for
sure, but which part of this is crazy, exactly? By this logic, you
are crazy too, Gramma. You are raising me even now. You are the
third parent in our now splintered household.

it was never really about Black Jesus (no offense)
it was the car rides in Grandma's Dodge Dynasty
it was the home-cooked meals and red punch in the church basement

after service, i'd check my face in the mirror, count how many
red lips dapped my cheekbones—look how big i'm getting—
don't i look just like Joycetta, especially in the eyes

5

it was the odd comfort of being in a room full of people who knew
my history before i learned their names, who already loved me
because i belonged to her

In one recording I took, it's your birthday and we're all going around saying things we love about you. My sister, the heavy sleeper, describes your style of parenting as "tough love." She remembers how you used to wake her up by pinching her nose shut, so as to make sure she wouldn't be late to school. Another sibling says, "You always pick up the phone." My youngest sister says, "You are the most consistent person I know." I say, "You don't just teach us things; you show us." We say, "We love you, Gramma. You say, "I love you all too. Now turn that thing off!"

Grandma J's the reason why i sing the way i do. the steady organ hum
under a deacon's prayer. i hum "Never Would Have Made It" to the sweet
potatoes in my new kitchen pot, hoping they taste like hers. she used to
hold my hand when we sang it. Grandma of Lasalle, Grandma of the
usher board. Grandma knowing every word, loudest in the pew.

My favorite story you tell is the one where you are five years old and you are riding your horse, Molly, through a cornfield on the way to somebody's house. It's late at night or early in the morning, and you fall asleep on the horse and slide off. By some miracle the horse doesn't trip over you or trample you. She gets down on her knees and bends her neck down so you can reach up, grab onto her mane, and climb back on. Every time I hear this story I think, *Wow, that horse loved you.* It feels like the beginning of a movie about a little Black girl who speaks to horses, who saves her family from some great threat using this special power.

i'm a crate digger, thumbing through her old records.
who would i be without my shovel? what would my voice sound like?
where would my gravity come from? cooking with Grandma's recipes
will never taste the same. but one day my grandchildren may taste
what i made and call it the original. they won't know any better.

I keep asking you to tell me stories about Arkansas, about your childhood, because I am in awe of how many lives one person can live in one lifetime. You were a bank teller, a meter maid, an usher board member, a caretaker for five grandchildren, a postal worker who hid a bottle of liquor in your boot and played bid whist with coworkers, a restaurant owner in Mississippi with Grandaddy. When I was born you shuttered its doors and drove up north to be my grandmother. I am so honored that you chose coparenting me as one of your many lives. I can't help that you're my muse, that every river in me runs back to you.

poetry is all about economy, fit.
i have been writing the same poem
over and over again in different words.
i love you. i love you. i love you.

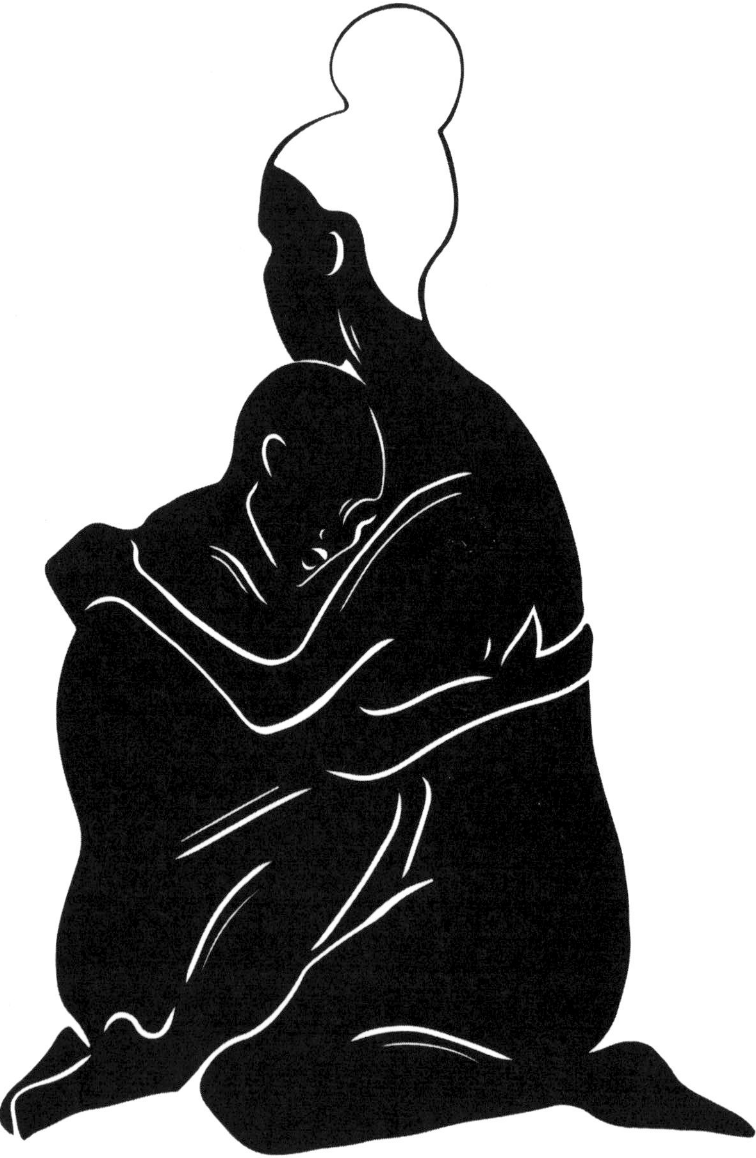

I LOVE YOU, BABY

BY TEMBE DENTON-HURST

was in the back of an Uber when he told me you were on the way. Careening headfirst into the Midtown Tunnel, iPhone pressed to my head and lips pressed together. He was at Sharif's swim practice, and although he didn't say it, I knew he was working. Just like he did when I was little and he would take us to the pool. His thick ream of papers now replaced by a clunky work laptop.

At first, he tried to play coy. "I have to talk to you this weekend," he said, my heart firmly in my throat. Never tell me that you want to talk later unless you want me to have a heart attack. I pressed, like I always do, pushing him to reveal whatever was to be revealed immediately.

"Okay, but don't tell your sister," he insisted. I agreed. My sister, our sister, has a tendency to take things personal. She was also on vacation, and he knew, before I did, that this would be the kind of destabilizing news that would make her want to come home. My initial conclusion was that he was getting married, which, given the shakiness of his voice, an always steady voice as you now know, should have tipped me off that this was a bad guess. I kept my prediction to myself, let him go first.

"Di Di's pregnant."

I inhaled sharply. "Are you serious? How far along is she?"

"Three months."

I quickly did the math. I tried not to cry.

I met your mom a few months before. It was a rare Thanksgiving/family reunion mashup, where Hurst-Gersts from around the country descended on an Embassy Suites in Alexandria, Virginia, wearing Day-Glo orange T-shirts and relearning each other's names. They showed up late, after dinner, him in his three-quarter zip pullover and her in matte black rain boots. I approached with caution. I had two missions to complete. The first was to meet your mom and get a feel for her energy. The second was to get him to speak to Connay, whom he'd been pretending not to know for the past four years, despite knowing I've loved her since then. It was uneventful—a hello, goodbye, and awkward side hug. She was quiet. Navigating my second mission took up much of my time, so stressful that by the end of the night, I was taking desperate pulls from a vape in a suite across the hall.

"So what does this mean?" I asked the man on the phone, who was both my father and now someone else's. Ours. But it didn't feel that way then. It felt like the pieces of my life were dislodging, twisting and stretching me against my will. What would Mommy say? What would Nace think? I said a lot of mean things next. Things I won't bring up because when I look at you now, all I see is sunshine in your bright eyes and love everywhere else. I want you to know that I came around quickly, and after the frustration, tears, and anxiety, I realized you and I were always meant to be.

"She could be your daughter," he told me next, and I, at twenty-two, felt a sort of panic that brought me face-to-face with my mortality in a way I didn't expect.

I would always watch you from this distance, an adult distance that would make me sister but also authority. It was different with Nace. She and I, eighteen months apart, grew alongside each other, facing life at the same breathtaking pace. We were *the girls*. A unit. TembeNace. No space. We would go on imaginary vacations to Vegas and Hawaii from our tiny apartment on East 18th Street, turning our tiny underwear into bikini tops and lounging beneath the shade of pulled-out dresser drawers. We would argue about what belonged to who, only ever agreeing that we belonged to each other. We were sisters, and this is the way I knew sisters to be. We spoke the same language, punctuated by messy, inaccurate patois, jokes about Daddy's mumble-drone, and a shared love for playing dolls. You and I would speak different languages, my experience so far from yours. We would know him differently too. He loved me first, and so he did it imperfectly but would love you last and maybe more carefully. I wondered, even then, what would bind us, how we would relate. If we could ever be close.

I'd dreamt you a few nights before knowing you without realizing it. You, all chocolate and sunshine, sat dutifully in the bathtub while I bathed your deep bronze skin, cleaning the folds and crevices. You stared up at me with those brilliant, dark eyes and smiled, mouth stretched wide. We looked alike. I didn't know what it meant. I called Mommy the next morning, who, despite always having the answers had none, and went on about my day unknowingly. But then I knew what I couldn't un-know. Which is that you were coming whether I liked it or not, and that I'd have to make room.

When I saw your mother next, she barely looked pregnant. The evidence of your arrival scared me most, but I asked to touch the belly anyway. I felt you then, a hard, unmoving bump cloaked in a vaguely patriotic T-shirt. It was the Fourth of July. The word "family" lost its shape soon after. What once meant me, Mommy, Daddy, Nace, and Sharif now included you and Di Di, and Connay too. We were expanding by force. You pushed our father most of all. He, with his expectations and declarations, had decided long ago that I, his firstborn, was destined for a life with clear-cut names for all the things that I am. Instead, he got something messier. But you softened him in that way that new babies do. First, his stomach grew rounder to match your mother's, undoing his two-a-day gym workouts and endless hours of spin class. He even let that honey-colored girl that calls you "best friend" and I call "baby" stay at the house. That's progress. We made progress.

And then suddenly there you were. Real flesh and blood. Gray, like fresh Black people are. I watched you from a screen four hundred miles away, clutching Connay excitedly and zooming in on your little features. They named you Tasmin Zarah, a play on Tazewell and Sarah, our grandparents. I rushed down to meet you a few days later, zipping down I-95 in our Nissan Sentra, the wind carrying us home. We were on a mission—the one that would unite you and me.

Your mom brought you to me like a present, wrapped and swaddled in a blanket with your little head buried inside. You were so small. So new. So wrinkly. I cooed and oohed and ahhed. I settled you in the crook of my elbow, and your dark eyes blinked open to look at me. I kissed you. I knew we now shared everything, you and me. Blood, breath, and body.

LOVES

BY NADIA OWUSU

Scrolling through my phone, I found a photograph of the three of us at a years-ago cocktail party. We're dressed for work, so I assume it was at some dull conference, but we're dancing—our arms reaching, our knees bent, our faces exuberant. Around us, a few people I don't recognize—all of them white—stand stiffly, drinking red wine. A woman with a careful blonde blowout watches us, her pale eyes wide with surprise.

In those days, we'd take our lunches out to the park. We'd sit in the sun and analyze power: Who did we need to move, and how far? What would it take? Who were our allies and opponents? We were trying to change an institution, trying to hold it to its stated values and mission, trying to get more resources to Black people who were assembling a more caring future with their bare hands. We were trying, as June Jordan put it, to "contribute to the positive changing of the world."

Well, alongside others, we did move the institution. We moved money. Then, one by one, we left, exhausted, and the money was reverted. The institution regressed. Did we fail? Perhaps. But, looking at that photograph of us, I recalled three sentences in Toni Morrison's *Beloved* containing a lovely and profound expression of love. About the woman he traveled thirty miles for, just to bid her good morning, Sixo says: "She is a friend of my mind. She gather me, man. The pieces I am, she gather them and give them back to me in all the right order." *A friend of my mind.* Just thinking those words softens me.

Early in the pandemic when I was hardened by fear, on the internet, I came across a 1960 photograph by Roy DeCarava of jazz greats John Coltrane and Ben Webster embracing. Webster, eyes closed, forehead creased with focus, has one arm around Coltrane's shoulder, drawing him even closer, tighter. Coltrane's eyes are also closed. His nose is pressed against Webster's chin. Both are smiling sweetly. A hint of a dimple interrupts Coltrane's cheek.

Friends of the mind, I thought.

Another photograph I love: James Baldwin and Nina Simone sit side by side on a sofa. She wears a straight bobbed wig. He holds a cigarette between two fingers in a raised hand. Their bodies are angled toward each other. Her expression is serious, her mouth open, mid-speech. He gazes at her with a mischievous expression, like he's coming up with a good retort. *Friends of the mind.*

My loves, I will always remember the ripe pleasure of conspiring with you in the afternoon sun, the thrill of co-creating small but tangible shifts, the joy of dancing together against decorum. All of that, I carry with me. What I mean is: You are my sisters and comrades, friends of my mind. What I mean is: You changed me irreversibly. What I mean is: Let's go dancing somewhere inappropriate as soon as we can.

Nadia

A LOVE LETTER TO MY HAIR

BY JOY-ANN REID

This is a love letter to my coarse, unmanageable, unpredictable Black hair.

ello, love. I can call you *love* today because I have learned to love you. And that has taken a lifetime. When we were young together, you were my challenge and my silent enemy. You were infuriating and frustrating and altogether wrong. I wanted you to be long and blonde, like Farrah Fawcett's; like the hair the white women in the Breck commercials on TV tossed back while in the shower or walking down the street, or tall like my Afros on my favorite dancers on *Soul Train*. Or glorious and hanging down my back like Diana Ross. But you were quite the opposite of all that. So I would throw a towel over the top of you to pretend I was in *Charlie's Angels*; or endure the hot comb and the Blue Magic grease that singed my scalp where the comb met my edges because I wanted you to be "good hair." Because that's what I was told was beautiful.

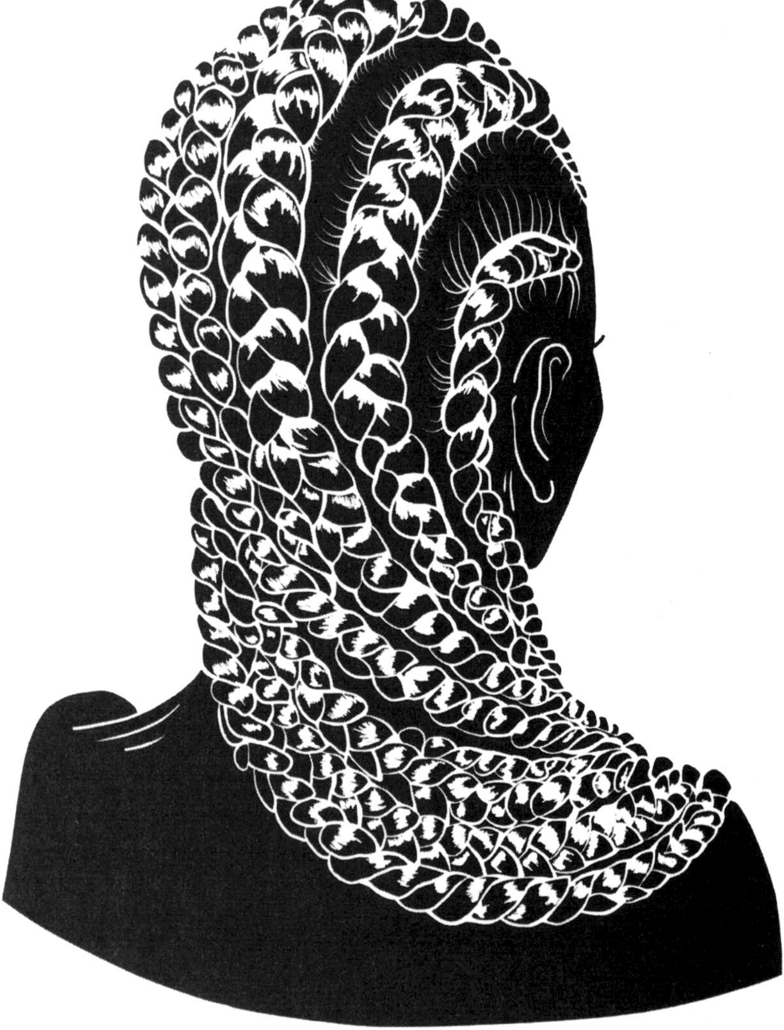

There were mixed girls at school who had hair like I wanted, and I quietly envied them. And it hit hard when they or their friends mocked me because you were too short and too coarse and too "nappy." But I trained myself not to care because I was a sporty-nerdy girl, and you were the hair that sporty-nerdy girls had. By college, I became intensely defensive of you, especially when my white roommates or even complete strangers would try to touch you without my permission just out of "curiosity." I mean, *How does it stand up like that?! It's SO AMAZING. Can I touch it??? I wish my hair did those things . . .* Cue my unfriendliest look and a nasty reply, which was ironic because my first name literally has "joy" in it. Because the answer was *NO.* And also *fuck off,* because this is Harvard, not the human zoo.

By the time I graduated, I had learned to chemically tame you; to cut you into Halle Berry and Nia Long styles; to get you braided so you hung as long as I wanted or weaved into any style I pleased. And I embraced the versatility of you, whether cornrowed or piled high on my head or laid, curled, and swept to the side—YOU, my hair love—are indeed amazing. You are amazing in ways that African things can uniquely be—resilient and strong and adaptable. And unstoppable.

And so, looking back on all that you have been and done and how you have challenged and infuriated but also defined me, and my Africanness and my Guyaneseness and my Black Girlness, I have fallen quite fully in love with you and would love you even if you were all gone away, leaving nothing but bald badness behind. Because no matter what else you are, you are mine and you are me, even when you are completely on my nerves. You are Blackness. And Black is beautiful.

With learned love,
Joy

A QUEER KIND OF LOVE

BY BILQUISU ABDULLAH

I want to be loved.
Loved like no other.
Unique and fluid
wouldn't begin to describe it.
That's the kind of love
I hold for others.
The kind that invades me
so strangely.
Crawls
into the walls
of my chest.
Runs deep with sorrow
and longing.

I want a love so sharp,
it cuts me so deep.
And in its absence
is where I would crumble.

I want a staring contest
in a lavender lilac field.

I want soft caresses
outlining my body.

I want to be wrapped
in a blanket of your
soft, warm, dark voice.

I want to sit in a park
with frigid hands in my pockets
and think of you.

I want something to pray
to the cosmos about.

I want effortless.
I want irrevocable.
I want unconditional.
I want limitless.
I want sparks.
I want tenderness
and soft grins.

And when I lie down to
take my forever nap,

I want to know that
I was loved.
And I want to know
that I have loved.

And that.
Is a queer kind of love.
My love.

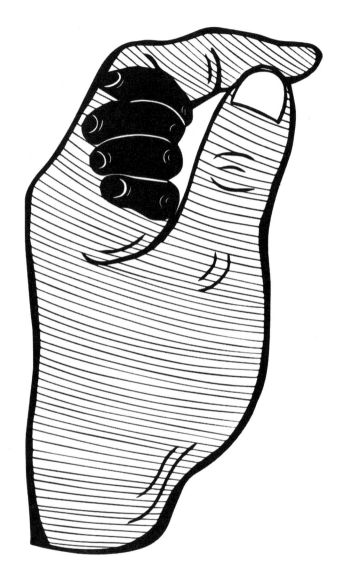

DEAR SKAI, ZOIE, AND BRAMMIE

BY RAKIA REYNOLDS

I carry you with me everywhere I go.

Not just your photos and videos on my phone—so many photos and videos—or the sounds of your voices swirling around in my head or the memories we create daily. My perfectly flawed body is a reminder of *my why*, of my absolute adoration for you.

My scars—relics of your birth—itch daily. Whether on a call, in a meeting, or making dinner, the skin around my midsection yearns to be scratched. And when my nails relieve the itch, I am instantly transported back to the time when I first heard each of your cries; I smell the sweetness of you, just moments old, and recall the feeling of your tiny mouth as I nursed you.

Each time I do jumping jacks, trying to fool myself that I am once again a PYT, my sciatic nerve reminds me this body is not what it once was. When I deign to run alongside you, my knees hasten my steps, remembering the days that I lifted strollers up and down stairs, shuttling your beautiful brown bodies around town. The other day someone noticed that I had a little dip on my right side, which made me recall how I carried all three of you on my hip at all hours of the day and night, close enough to feel your heartbeat on my arm, your precious heads on my shoulder.

I embrace these reminders of what I've experienced and how joy has been abundantly present throughout my life. Our bodies remember everything, whether psychological, spiritual, mental, or physical. If they happened ten minutes or ten years ago, those experiences are imprinted on us.

I will never stand up straight like a cadet or have perfect posture like a ballet dancer. There are no marathons in my future. Ironman/woman competitions? Forget about it. And that is fine. It's beautiful, actually. Because you, my dear, talented, funny, altruistic children, are worth every dip in my hip.

Your birth has given me the greatest gift—a reminder of whom I was put on this Earth to serve.

Skai, Zoie, and Brammie, through my service to you as your mother, I have blossomed in unimaginable ways. Not only do I have the divine responsibility and honor of being your mother but I also get to help other people grow and glow. My personal and work relationships have grown stronger because of my service in raising you. When a friend is in need, I can hold space for their pain, sorrow, and joy. When a client needs direction, I am able to lead strategies to help them achieve success. I was born with these gifts, but your birth activated them on a different level.

My body always remembers you. Your laughter lives in each step I take and every strategic vision I execute. When I greet the sun, stretching to welcome its rays and feel a tweak in my side, I smile, knowing that all three of my loves are *my why.*

Love always,
Mom

LETTER TO MY UNBORN NIECE

BY AKILI KING

I already know I have a new best friend.
You've already made me want to be better, and you haven't
said a word.
That's how I know you are going to be powerful.

The world might knock you down, but I'm here to pick you
back up.
My trauma and pain will not be in vain, as my lessons have
turned into wisdom that I will pass on to you and to my future
child as well.

When you don't feel beautiful, I'm here to remind you
that beauty is whatever you say it is and that it comes from
within.

When you feel you're not enough, I'm here to remind you
your cup is full and spilling over.

When you feel like giving up, I'm here to tell you that taking breaks is okay and part of the process of achieving a goal and not to feel discouraged.

When your heart is broken, it's a reminder that you are human and have the capacity to love again.

When you feel fear, I'm here to remind you that your greatest fears block you from your own superpowers.
I will gently say, "Get out of your own way."

And when you feel alone, know you're loved without a word having to be said—just the way you reminded me that life is filled with so much beauty and joy to look forward to.

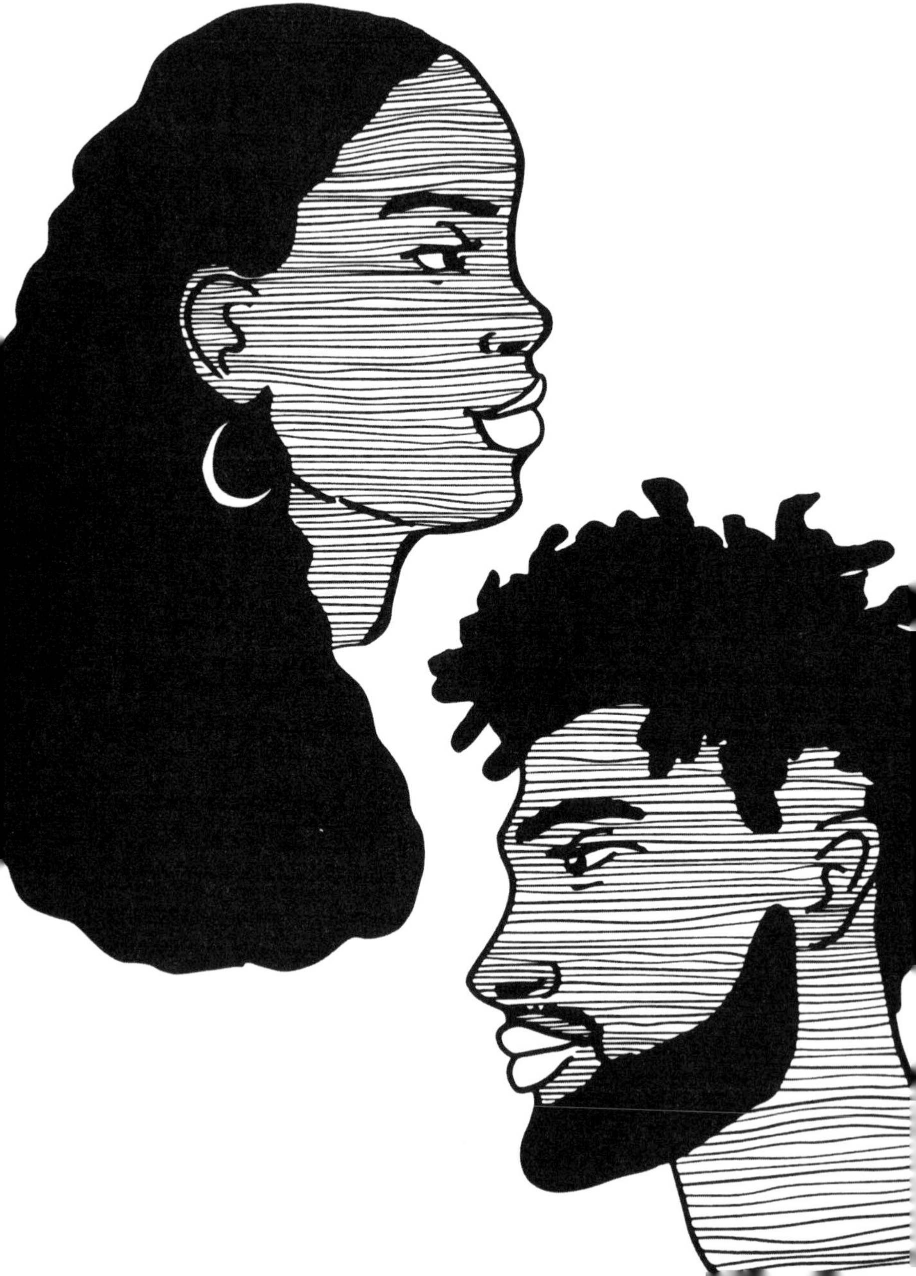

TO DIMPLES

BY JOEL CASTÓN

DIMPLES,

t's 6:12 in the morning, and I'm tossing and turning waiting for your call. I prefer it this way, no longer confined to a bed with my legs hanging off the end, arms asleep from the restriction. It's hard to spread out on a prison bunk.

It was during those moments—my darkest and bleakest—that you appeared in my life as an angel. The perfume on your letters gave me strength to wake up, to leave the iron bars that held me captive, to make my morning call. Now, it is you who calls me.

I never knew love like this before. I marvel at the strength you had to care for someone you had only first met through letters. The impression of the ink of your pen told a story. The intonation of your penmanship spoke in your stead. The smiley faces that you drew were my kisses.

Now, I am blessed by your presence. Long gone are the fifteen-minute phone calls that haunted us with each passing second, the guards who subjected you to strip searches just to see me in person, telling you what to wear and where to sit. Now,

I can walk freely in the shopping store with you. I'm like a shadow on your hip. I can't help but stare at you and tell you over and over again that I love you for loving me at times when I found it difficult to even love myself.

Te amo, mi amor.
Joel

MY DEAREST KEN

BY BARBARA EDELIN

I saw a rainbow today. I know it was you smiling at me. Sometimes I see a cardinal fly by and land outside my window and I know it's you, or when I can't remember something important and somehow, I find it in a file or folder. I know it's you showing me where to go, as you always did whenever I was unsure or floundering. You gave me direction and support. You were always there, and now you're not.

This is not what we said our life together would be. We said we'd grow old together, and we laughed when we agreed that I'd wipe the drool from your lip when you were ninety-five and I was eighty-four. We never thought about death or one of us leaving the other.

When we first met on a blind date on a cold January day in Boston, we both knew instantly that we were meant to be together. They say "you know" when the "right one" comes along, and we both knew.

You were so handsome! I was speechless when you walked into a crowded Super Bowl party and we were introduced. I had no idea you would take my breath away in that single moment, but you did!

You were so funny and clever and wise—all things I realized in those first few moments. I knew you were meant for me. We both had complicated lives at the time, and it would be three years before we somehow circled back and rediscovered each other, single and available. Funny how life makes a way for the things that are truly meant to be. For us, it was predetermined that we would find each other.

You reminded me of my dad, who was my male role model growing up. A strong, determined Black man. Dedicated to service in our community on the South Side of Chicago and so dedicated to his family. His love for my mom, my sisters, and me was my foundation. My father was everything to me growing up. When I married you, I had the same feeling of support and comfort that I felt my dad and mom had in their marriage. I felt so lucky to have found that kind of love with you.

Thirty-five years of a life of joy, excitement, and happiness. You gave me the two greatest gifts of my life—our children, Joseph and Corinne. Without them, I don't think losing you would be bearable. They are my rock and help me through the ebbs and flows of life without you.

Cancer took you from me, from us, way too soon. But I'm so thankful for the time we had. I love you now and always, my Ken. You're forever in my heart!

Barb

AWE

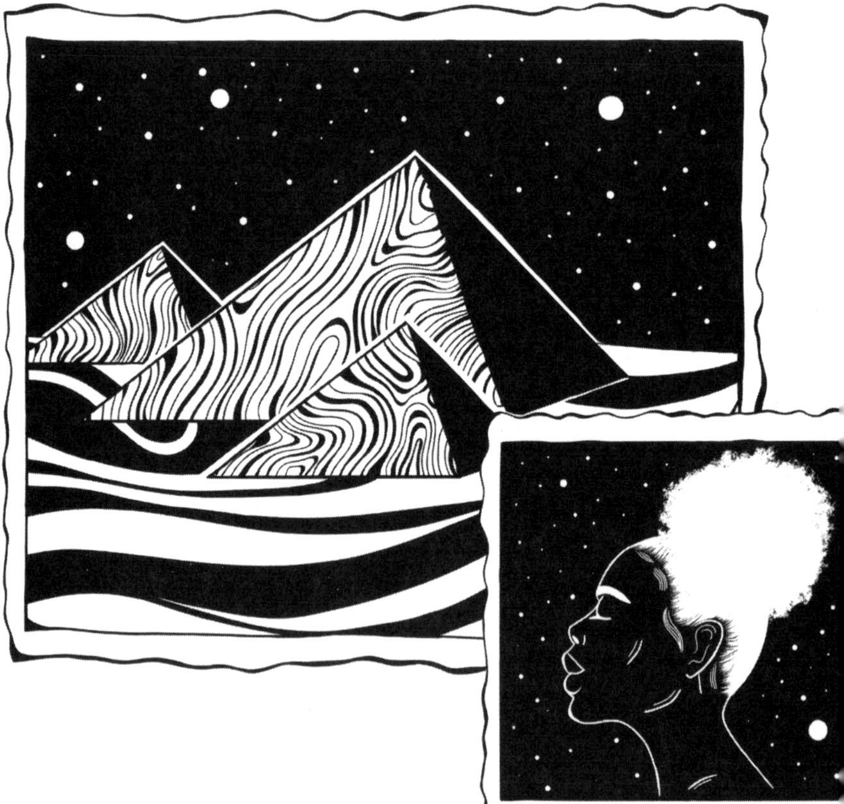

DEAR EGYPT

BY MORGAN JERKINS

I had dreamed of you many nights since I was a kid. Always considered an "old soul," I'd like to believe that those who deemed me as such were referring to my emotional intelligence or sage wisdom, but it was the part inside myself that leaned toward something as ancient as your waters and monuments. I do not know when my interest in you started. Perhaps it's when my mother bought me an illustrated book of your land in antiquity or when I watched a television adaptation of Cleopatra VII's life. Maybe when I read *The Royal Diaries* or when I watched *The Mummy* and idolized Evie for her brilliance even if she was unsure of herself amongst the men. I knew that you were calling out to me like a siren. Only I knew that if I answered you, I wouldn't suffer. On the contrary, I may return home larger than I ever thought possible.

It was the winter of 2019, and I was far away from friends and family in Germany where I was teaching for part of a semester. A bank holiday was approaching, which meant that I only taught one day in that particular week. I wrestled with the thought of coming to you. I had been dumped just a few months before I left for Europe. Emotionally devastated, exhausted, fearful, and shaken up, I didn't think it would be right for me to see you. I had always imagined visiting your museums and pyramids with a partner, not by myself. But you were only six hours away by flight from Munich. I had the money. But most importantly, I had the freedom. Every person whom I confided in told me that I needed to go.

So I did.

I sat at my gate and then on the plane wondering what the hell I was thinking. Was I making a huge mistake? I should've never done this alone.

I arrived a little past midnight, and the next morning, I saw that my room overlooked the Nile. I had never gazed upon anything so old before. Then I saw the Giza pyramids, the Valley of the Kings, Hatshepsut's Temple, the Temple of Karnak, and Alexandria. I healed no matter which direction I turned. Fresh air re-energized all my emotions each time a new sight astounded me. I returned to being a child. I recognized my vulnerability as a human being as I walked down hallways and pathways of mud, stone, or sand that reminded me of how small yet precious I was in the face of immense architecture. I returned yet again to being this woman I am today who had the bravery to give herself the greatest gift she has given so far.

There are still some nights I think of you with disbelief. I do not know how I was able to immerse myself in your space for just a few days: resting on a boat moving along the Nile, drinking an

Egyptian mango drink, getting henna done along the banks of the Mediterranean. I do not know how I had the audacity.

But I am glad that I satisfied my decades-long curiosity of you. I'm glad I never have to wonder if you are really as good as the white men who wrote about you said you were. You are better. Because I got to experience you for me and only me.

Our memory together is one that will sit in the history books of my own heart. Our memory together is one that no one can ever take away from me.

JUSTICE MARSHALL

BY BEN CRUMP

I still remember my first peek beyond the vast veil of race that cut across my North Carolina town like the Great Wall. Fourth grade. In 1954, you told my town that it must integrate its schools "with all deliberate speed." Twenty-five years later, we were still working on the project, trying to get the mix right. That day, I walked beside my momma to a bus stop just down the block, passing all manner of refuse on the way. Dilapidated homes collapsing into themselves. School buildings shedding lead paint. Forgotten car bodies sitting on bricks. She sat me on the bus and wished me well on my first day at my new school.

The bus shuttled me across the tracks to the other side where everything sparkled. The grass was mowed, and the pages in the textbooks were crisp. All the white kids wore their new outfits. They'd never seen a car on bricks before.

When I got home, I complained to Momma. I asked her why they had it so good when we didn't have a pot to piss in or a window to throw it from. I asked if it'd always been like this.

She told me that discussions between men in a marble building a world away put me on that bus. She told me about a court case I'd never heard of: *Brown v. Board of Education*. She told me about you.

I barely knew what a civil rights attorney was, but I knew that a civil rights attorney showed me a side of life I might've never seen otherwise. And that was all I needed to know. I decided that day that I would become one.

You don't know what you started, sir.

I worked hard in school, graduated from Florida State University, then began the work. I'd been an attorney for a few years before anyone heard my name for the first time. It was attached to the name "Martin Lee Anderson." A fourteen-year-old boy died while incarcerated at a youth detention center in Florida. While he lay on the ground, officers punched and kicked him, then covered his mouth and made him sniff smelling salts to no response. The whole thing played out on surveillance videotape. When he was pronounced dead, the officers blamed his sickle cell trait.

His case threw me into the fire of working toward justice before the public eye. When the work was done and the dust settled, we secured the largest payout for his family that the state of Florida had ever awarded. It wouldn't ease their pain, but it was a step toward justice.

There have been so many Martin Lee Andersons. So many Trayvons. I worked with many before and many since, the vast majority of whom died in anonymity, their names never becoming hashtags.

My fight against state violence is one that you took up first. We call it police brutality; in your day, it was lynching. Ida B. Wells said, "A Black man was lynched yesterday," and for every day she said it, she was right. The weight of all those names is a heavy load. So many of them will never see true justice, the same today as it was in your day.

Compartmentalization is key. You used to say, "Keep your eyes on the prize. Remain focused on the task." You were unflinching, unwavering in your pursuit of justice. You knew, like I know, that the moment you falter is the same moment that injustice finds room to flourish. So, we keep our heads up, our eyes trained on the horizon.

And amid tragedy, we recognize the small victories.

We made Trayvon Martin the number-one news story in the world in 2012. Finally, people paid attention to the Black death happening all around us. We secured a conviction for George Floyd's killer. We secured a conviction for Ahmaud Arbery's killers. Soon, Lord-willing, we'll secure a conviction for Breonna Taylor's killer—the first-ever conviction of an officer involved in the killing of a Black woman.

Every day, I sit with families in their darkest moments. I try to make sense of senseless events for them. I listen. And when it's my turn to speak, I never promise them an outcome. I promise them that I will do everything in my power to get to the truth. That is ultimately all I can control. Justice relies on the truth. And if I've done my job, in the end, justice follows.

I sued Harvard recently on behalf of a woman whose property it holds. The school keeps daguerreotypes of her enslaved ancestors in its archive—a father and daughter who were stripped naked and then poked and prodded to prove that Negroes were best suited for the field. She wants them back, and Harvard, recognizing their value, won't give 'em. We sued to make them.

Sir, you would have loved my opening statement.

I told them that I am many things, but above all, I am a free man. The reason I could stand before them as a free man was because, more than two hundred years ago, courageous men argued before that very court and made Massachusetts the first state to outlaw slavery. Then I asked whether they had that same courage.

When all was done, the court unanimously decided to deny the school's motion to dismiss. The woman will have her day in court.

I invoked the legacy of our vocation because I know that our vocation has meaning. Each person contributes to the struggle in their own way; each contribution is valuable. But ours is critical. We are on the front lines. The courtroom is the battlefield for the struggle. You taught me that.

The struggle is my calling, just as it was yours. Folks tend to condemn the struggle when really, they should celebrate it. I fell in love with it—there's no other way to do this work and keep alive. Progress is gratifying, but a mystery. The struggle is all that's guaranteed—like a car requires friction to start, progress demands struggle.

That's why I orient myself toward the struggle. I don't pray for easier times; I pray for stronger children. I pray that I can do for them what you did for me—light a path forward, show them the pleasure and power of struggle.

Sincerely,
Benjamin Crump, Esq.

ON BLACK LOVE . . .

BY LYNAE VANEE BOGUES

As an enthusiast of Black History, I am particularly indebted to the aspect of Black Love. After rigorous study, interrogation, and observation of moments, movements, and figures, it is my belief that the most political thing you can do is love another Black person. It's an act of resistance. It is revolutionary.

Moments, movements, and figures in Black History have all had the common goals of freedom and equity. The common method of operation throughout has been the use of identity politics. And truly, any identity politics is only successful when assigned value. And Black Love has been the only base offering support for the conviction that Black life, in all its forms, is valuable and worth moving for.

Black Love is a broad-sweeping concept that exists in various forms: mother to child, lover to lover, friend to friend. It can be administered in a multitude of ways, sure. But it does hold a unique and uniform set of characteristics that gives it a distinct shape.

Black Love is inspired by colorful epithets and euphemisms, requiring the prerequisite of our shared cultural experience. It

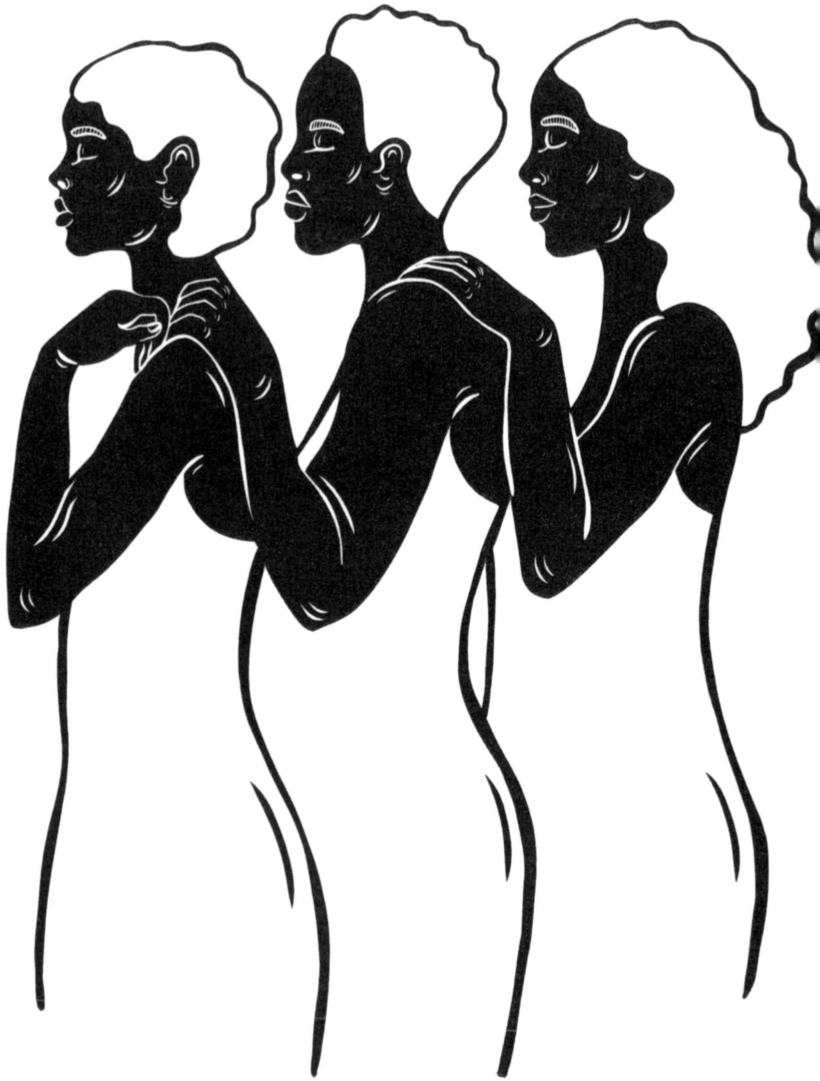

is an amalgamation of intimate head nods and gestures only understood if you went to the same school. It is imbued with jazz, meaning it has a rhythm you can't help but dance to—one that forces you to ride it with little to no direction, and quite frankly, everybody can't play it. It is a very particular thing that belongs to a very particular club, and if you did not pledge, you simply won't understand. And though the unfortunate reality is that many of us were hazed in the process, when you think about it, Black Love is how we survive.

White people have the luxury of experiencing love as a journey only burdened with the defaults of humanity. However, we experience love as an escape. It is a fort we build to shield the people we love from oppression and where we take ourselves to be repaired. The people we love are our safe zones. They allow us to direct our attention away from the veil and into the worlds we build together. When two or three of us gather to love or be loved, it is already implied that each of us had to work through a thing even to offer such an extension of ourselves, which makes our love stronger.

So when I think about Black Love, I am enamored with it. I think of the haven it provided Black men, women, and children when faced with violence. I think of the agency it provided Black people when they were presumed not to have choices. I think of the sacrifices; how, when no one else would dare, we thought highly enough of one another to show up . . . to fight for a better tomorrow.

I think my favorite iterations of Black Love are:

The praying hands of grandmothers.

The taste of watermelon cracked on the back of country pickup trucks.

The arms of big sisters who held emotional baby brothers.

The desires of men who have mended women's overrun gardens.

Strong people who did not need strong leaders.

Maybe most

When applied to self.

Or

When finding love is all that matters.

I love Black Love because, when done in earnest and done *right*, it is possibly the most healing thing you can experience.

Lynae Vanee

JAZZ

BY DICK PARSONS

Elizabeth Barrett Browning framed the question best: *How do I love thee?* I love the way you make me feel. You transport me to a place where troubles melt like lemon drops and the worries of my day-to-day world are suspended. You clear my mind and quench my thirst for beauty. You make me feel young again. And you swing!

I recently asked my wife if I should take up meditation so I can achieve true peace of mind. She said, "You don't need to meditate; you have your music. When you are listening to it, you're someplace else; you're at peace." She knows best; you are my ultimate source of solace.

Ella, Sarah, Carmen, Nancy, Etta, Dinah, Diana, Diane, I would marry each of you if you would only promise to sing me to sleep every night (and were polygamy legal). Duke, Miles, John, Stan, Oscar, Erroll, Art, Paul, Wynton, I wish we could all hang out together. You and your colleagues in music are the apostles of my religion. Through your creativity and artistry, you restore my soul.

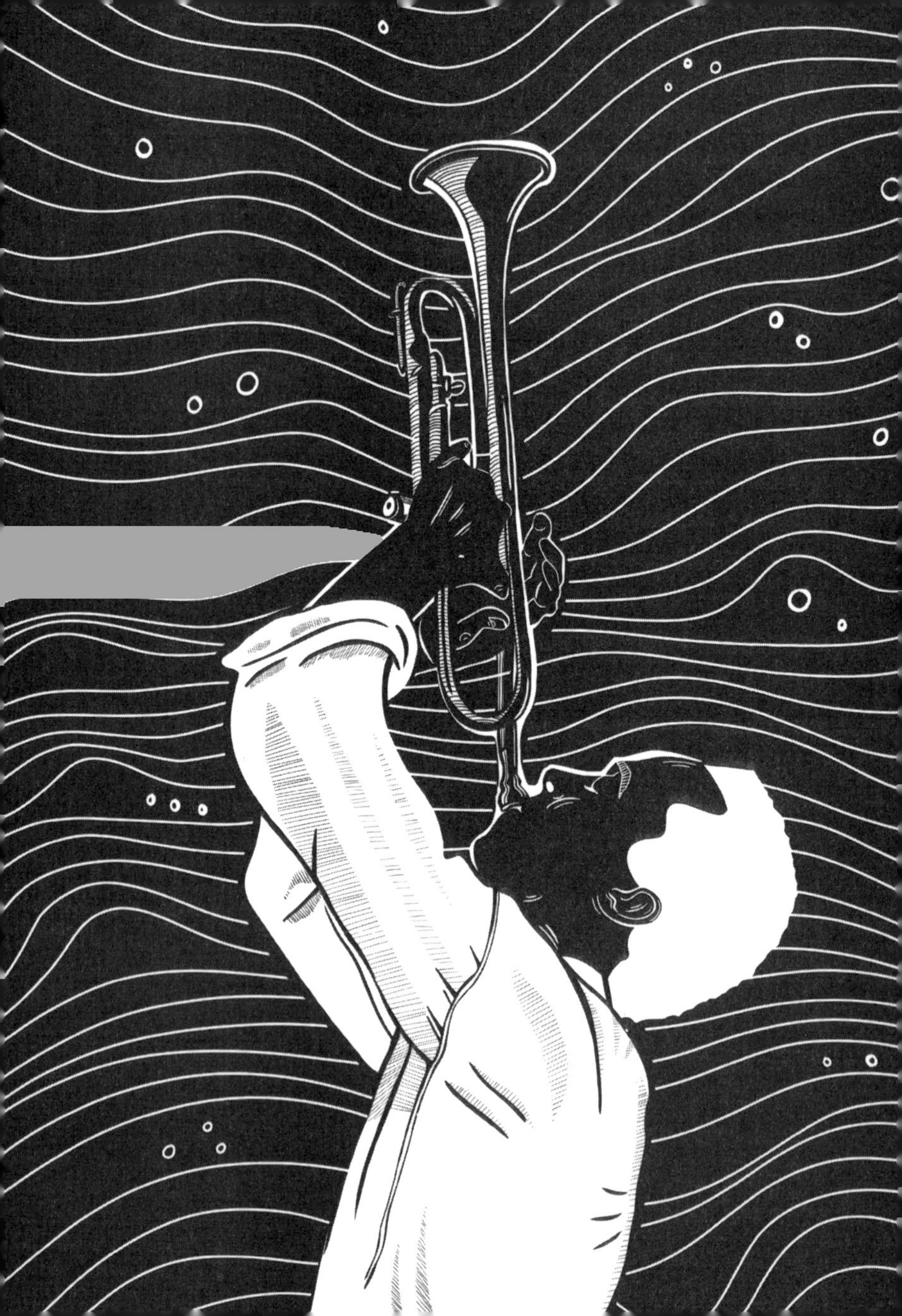

You are America's first and finest contribution to global culture, recognized and enjoyed around the world because of the universality of your rhythms, beats, and melodies. And I particularly love the fact that you originated from—and were nurtured by—the African-American community, my community. With all the focus of late on the horrors and deprivations visited on our people, I take enormous pride in the fact that we created you. You embody the best of us. The whole world listens to and enjoys our music.

There is no way I could give back what you have given me. The best I can do is help keep you alive to share with others. One small step I have taken in that direction is the restoration of Minton's Playhouse, the legendary house of jazz in Harlem. Minton's is now at the vanguard of clubs, bringing you to old and new audiences alike.

So, yes, in the words of Ms. Browning, *I love thee to the depth and breadth and height my soul can reach* . . . and then some. You are my salvation.

Dick Parsons

DEAR BLACK-ASSED RASP

BY DOUGLAS KEARNEY

What you do when you put that work in, you turn(t) singing to sangin', on some screwed-up face to come get to the sound. Wracked lovely, you come around to steady rattle the fashion from form, to disavow cuteness for raw greatness, for the big B Beauty of voice that means to be more, for the stretch that slow grinds with strain.

Your mess better than perfect, oh salty Black-assed Rasp.

Listen to you distressing what's polished, pushing what's posh, rioting prim notes to throat mosh. Pit the pit of the stomach with the spit of the gullet, the bucket of blood plus the sweat-christened pulpit. You play the *too high to get over* of trying to get over because of the way you shake me back into my skin, down the hole into my flesh, embodying melody, making it real and killing it, insisting each time on the expense of transcendence.

When you throttle vibrato, my eyes roll holy.

I hear your audio smoke pass dark lips, breaking the safety glass to throw away the extinguisher. You set the tune to burn in my ear, singeing singing signing its name across my mind and heart with a black finger. Soot my soul on down to cinders when you stoke it good-like. The sweat pop, the purl, the tear a fugitive out my eyes till my eyes shut the fire up in me.

Black-Assed Rasp, I mean to hold what's too hot to handle.

Got me like *unnngh*!

Got me like *oooof*!

Got me like *yeeesssss*!

I said, *Your mess work better than perfect, salty Black-assed Rasp.*

'Ey. Recall I was once a choirboy, trained to sing like a crystal bell. My uvula on some clapper clambering the second alto ringing out me, the notes taut to peal from a ruffed collar; ruffed collar like a sound bow. Pretty—what it was how we did it, arranged all neat and straight, pickets in a fence. Had that German, that Latin chiming out. Had that Greek that one time, shouting out from offstage, and even our shouts more knell than yell, had us some *technique*, had us pouring simple syrup, clear as that and sweet, that pretty tone.

Rasp, they ain't want you in there and you ain't want to come, so wasn't no use putting an ear out for you there.

But at home!

That's where I had heard you in the Drifter's leads, the sand grain still speckling crooners who refused cooled smoothness. Aretha's granular ascensions and descents, her silicate coruscation constellating black sky. James's nigh strident storm hits. Chaka's hollers: caustic, elastic. Wilson's wicked indelicate insistence. The harsh-gorgeous trajectories of Tina's highs.

You, the deliverer of hurt's texture, fluent in pain's rough tongues. When I work to make you mine, I want you to pour me heavy brown liquor sonics that shape-shift me to the bottle, the vessel.

Rasp, you rasped my voice, took your time at it, now my head-tone knappy and fine. When I hear you, Rasp, I know I'm fixing to be broken. I get up to get down. Taste the sweet in your salt. I'm quick to say, *Take your time. I came to be taken away.* To respond to the Black-assed noise in your Black-assed signal's call.

Black-Assed Rasp: your mess ever work better than perfect.

Love,
DK

LOVE LETTER TO THE BLACK CHURCH

BY MICHAEL ERIC DYSON

DEAR BLACK CHURCH,

Perhaps my love for you began when Sunday school teachers stooped down to hug me and plant motherly kisses on my four-year-old cheeks. It grew as they taught me a year later to recite from memory set pieces about Jesus loving all the children of the world on Easter Sunday. It deepened as gray-haired women, weathered by bitter experience and seasoned by suffering, testified at Wednesday night prayer service that God had been good to them through it all—disloyal and often fleeing men, disobedient children, pestering neighbors, cranky coworkers, gossiping fellow believers, and backstabbing friends. Whatever they confronted, however bad it got, and however poorly they were treated, they kept going, and God kept making a way out of no way and kept rewarding their persistence with a peace of mind that not even they could fully explain. Often, one of these saintly sisters caught the Holy Ghost and danced their

delight—they didn't usually speak in tongues; we weren't that kind of church, erupting in Pentecostal fervor and lurching in esoteric prophecy. But believers often unleashed furious "hallelujahs" in praise of the Most High.

My Beloved Black Church, I love how you embrace inspiring styles of performance. I love how you rehearse holy order in tunefully whispered prayers, solemn hymns, and orchestral melodies. I love how you dramatize spiritual release in unashamed tears and uncensored emotions. I must confess, however, that it was pulpit speech that pricked my ears and made me fall most deeply in love with you. I was infatuated with the way such speech sounded and the way it sounded the depths of Black existence, the way it signaled moral intent with just a sigh, the way it did racial work in clever turns of phrases and in subtle shades of meaning, the way it anthologized a kaleidoscope of Black verbal invention at a moment's notice, the way it married truth and restless cultural inventory.

It all started when I listened to the Reverend C. L. Franklin, the widely revered past master of the chanted sermon, or the "whoop" as we called it in Black religious circles, whose albums I pulled from the busy shelves of my grandfather's farmhouse in rural Alabama. I was all of six or seven years of age, and instead of playing on acres of unruly grass that was grazed by an aging feeble horse, I drank in the hypnotic cadences and enchanting melodies of the preacher dubbed "The Man with the Million-Dollar Voice," a nod to both his oratorical virtuosity and his commercial appeal in marketing over seventy albums of recorded sermons. Ray Charles may have famously brought gospel to rhythm and blues, but he returned the favor of C. L. Franklin shouting the blues of his native Mississippi in the gospel pulpit, torching the dignified church lectern with orchestrated frenzy and surprising intellectual sophistication.

I was mesmerized by Franklin's gifts. He lifted stories from the Bible to urge Black political resistance; he raided sociology to expose the deceits of American race. He had a moan so sweet that it shamed misery into hiding. His musical speech resolved dramatically from a piercing tenor to a resounding baritone. His theological imagination brought ancient Rome to segregated America. He marched in June 1963 with Martin Luther King Jr. in my native Detroit before King set the world aflame in Washington two months later with his "I Have a Dream" speech.

My Cherished Black Church, if Franklin ignited my love for you, King deepened my passion. I was nine years old when the prophet from Sweet Auburn in Atlanta met his end on a desolate motel balcony in Memphis. My grandfather's portable record player had inspired me to save my coins from after-school work at a nursery to amplify a room of my own—well, a room shared with my older brother, Anthony—and I sent off for a 45-rpm recording that excerpted King's most famous orations. "If you want a moratorium on demonstrations, put a moratorium on injustice," King's voice rang in booming defiance in Chicago. I loved everything about him—his radiant brown skin, his voluptuous lips, his neatly brushed-back hair, his perfectly trimmed mustache, his diminutive size that, even in death, brought him closer in my mind to my height and world, and above all, his majestic way with words, words that spilled from his mouth like golden offerings to the god of rhetoric, unceasing and unapologetic eloquence in the service of truth and humanity and justice for Black folk.

King loved Black people and I loved him for it, posthumously at least; for I had never heard of him before he was murdered. I loved him even more fiercely because, in my youthful mind, that made up for not knowing him and loving him and adding to his legion of admirers and lovers when he lived and breathed and fought and sacrificed and gave up the ghost for us. I lived on the words he spoke to a nation perplexed by his devotion but which needed it as much as breath itself, a nation that knew his name but never really knew the distance he had traveled to take them further and deeper into a world they claimed to invent, but which, in truth, they scarcely knew, not in the way he was forced to know it; and his instrument of instruction, his vehicle of enlightenment, was his aching, throbbing, vital, life-giving words. I missed his words when he first said them, but when I listened after he was gone, I understood what he meant because I had heard words like them in churches where preachers spoke of a God who loves and forgives and demands justice and cannot abide the petty beliefs and determined hatreds on which our nation, at its worst, feeds.

Dearest Black Church, it was in one of your hallowed sanctuaries in the ghetto of Detroit that I first heard at the age of twelve the man who clarified my existence with his words of salvation—no, not primarily salvation from the wiles of the Devil and the temptations of the flesh but salvation from a life left uncontemplated in dangerous streets where the seductions of illicit goods beckoned and, for others of my peers, in hollow middle-class homes where material gain failed to satisfy the soul. The words of Frederick George Sampson were sublimely baroque, charting a path through byzantine structures of race and religion as he crafted sermons that explained our citizenship in the kingdom of God.

Sampson cut a striking figure at six feet four inches with a bush of wiry gray hair in his later years that staked out a slight Afro-puffed claim on either side of his cranium and met in the middle as a truce to the war for disappearing follicles. His speech was peppered with homespun expressions from his upbringing in Port Arthur, Texas—yes, the home of rap group UGK, composed of Bun B and the late Pimp C, a home they shouted into glory with the acronym PAT. Sampson had a formidable command of English poetry—on many a day we traded verses from Wordsworth, Tennyson, and Longfellow—and he was equally conversant with Black literature, European philosophy, and German theology. It showed in the pulpit as his considerable erudition echoed in long quotes from memory of W. E. B. Du Bois and Bertrand Russell.

The latter made more than one appearance in a Sampson homily as he lowered his voice to a whisper and recited for us words that the revered British man of letters had penned to his lover Constance Malleson on October 23, 1946, twelve years to the day before I was born. Russell spoke of great pain, and love, in his search for divinity. Sampson meditated on Russell's vast knowledge to insist that even brilliant minds must grapple with a higher power. He turned often to the poetry of Langston Hughes—one reason I was particularly gratified to receive the medal in his name from City College of New York—to portray a beleaguered but triumphant diaspora. Whether he cited Shakespeare or playwright Charles Gordone or theologian Paul Tillich, Sampson memorably lifted us to higher intellectual and moral ground.

Black Church, my love, I cannot deny that you have also greatly hurt me. When I was in my early twenties, I sought to ordain three women as deacons in a Baptist church I led, but you cast me from my pulpit—well, at least some of your ostensible representatives did; though, in agreeing to the belief that God moves in mysterious ways, I can make no greater claim to divine inspiration in disputing their decision than they did in evicting me. Not only have I watched women pummeled by the soulless hammer of patriarchy, but I have witnessed us embracing a theology of Black bodies that protests the deranged assault on Black lips, hips, legs, arms, and faces, even as we pitch in with white evangelicals to despise queer Blackness, a sort of Blackness, paradoxically, that has so often blessed the Black church in song and sermon.

But, Cherished Black Church, I am still here, hanging on, mostly because you gave me the language to know myself and to know the truth and to tell that truth to a world that remains fatally incurious about our philosophical depth and moral ambition. Thank you, Black Church; for, at your best, you met me like Jesus met the woman at the well, and instead of offering harsh rebuke or caustic lesson, he greeted her at her own level, right where she lived, emotionally and psychologically, to take her where she could have hardly anticipated she would ever be, and in the end, to a place where she finally understood she needed to be. Some call it salvation; I call it love. My Dearest Black Church, you have done this for me, and for that, I love you. Always.

BLACK LOVE AS GRACE

BY IMANI PERRY

There is a profound moment in Lorraine Hansberry's classic play *A Raisin in the Sun*. After the adult son of the Younger family, Walter Lee, squanders the money they intended to use for a home and his sister Beneatha's education, Beneatha lets loose and calls him nothing but a "toothless rat." Lena Younger, their mother, chastens her. She says, "When you starts measuring somebody, measure him right, child, measure him right. Make sure you done taken into account what hills and valleys he come through before he got to wherever he is."

Even though I feel Beneatha's rage, I have learned to listen to Mrs. Younger. It is a statement about love as a form of grace. At that moment, Walter Lee has failed the family. In his desperation to be successful, he disregarded his responsibility to loved ones. He is ashamed. Of course, he ought to be held accountable. He hears the truth of his mistakes from the people who love him the most. But the point is this: accountability doesn't mean that love dies.

It is easy to love someone when they have been perfectly sweet, responsible, and kind. But the true measure of love may be in its difficulty. Human beings are complicated and imperfect. And we, Black people, carry a heavier burden than many others. Given the intensity of the pressures we live with: worries about money, illness, work, stress, and of course the ever-present reality of racism, it is really hard work to maintain our ideal selves. We try and do succeed, but sometimes we also fail. Those failures are usually forgivable. If they are, after they've taken place, there's a process of getting back to being in right relation with each other. That requires trustworthiness. We must treat each other with dignity, tenderness, respect, and kindness. All of these are appropriate expectations. But this is also true: when we falter, when we fail, or even just when we lock horns, grace can be our saving grace. I want to honor that grace. I thank God that I have been loved through my worst moments. I have been selfish, unkind, and irresponsible at moments in my life. And yet I have always been loved deeply. I have learned as someone who stands in a powerful tradition of Black mothering, to give that grace to others, even when I am holding them accountable. It is one of the most important things that I hope to pass on to my sons and the many generations to follow: that amazing grace.

DEAR BLACK AMERICA

BY BELINDA WALKER

Yeah, I'm talking to you. I just want you to know, I love you. Yeah, yeah, I know life sometimes seems like some old blues lyrics. I know it feels like you were born with a target on your back, that the fool at the job is getting on your last nerve, that that sales lady/cab driver/grocery clerk is giving you the side eye, that you bust your ass every day and still get called lazy and everything still costs more than you got. Trust me, I know.

But trust, I still love you—

yeah, you with the doo rag and saggy pants,

you with the Howard sweatshirt and Martha's Vineyard decal

you with the baby on your hip chewing the hell out of a piece of gum

you climbing the corporate ladder, bringing up the next sister behind you

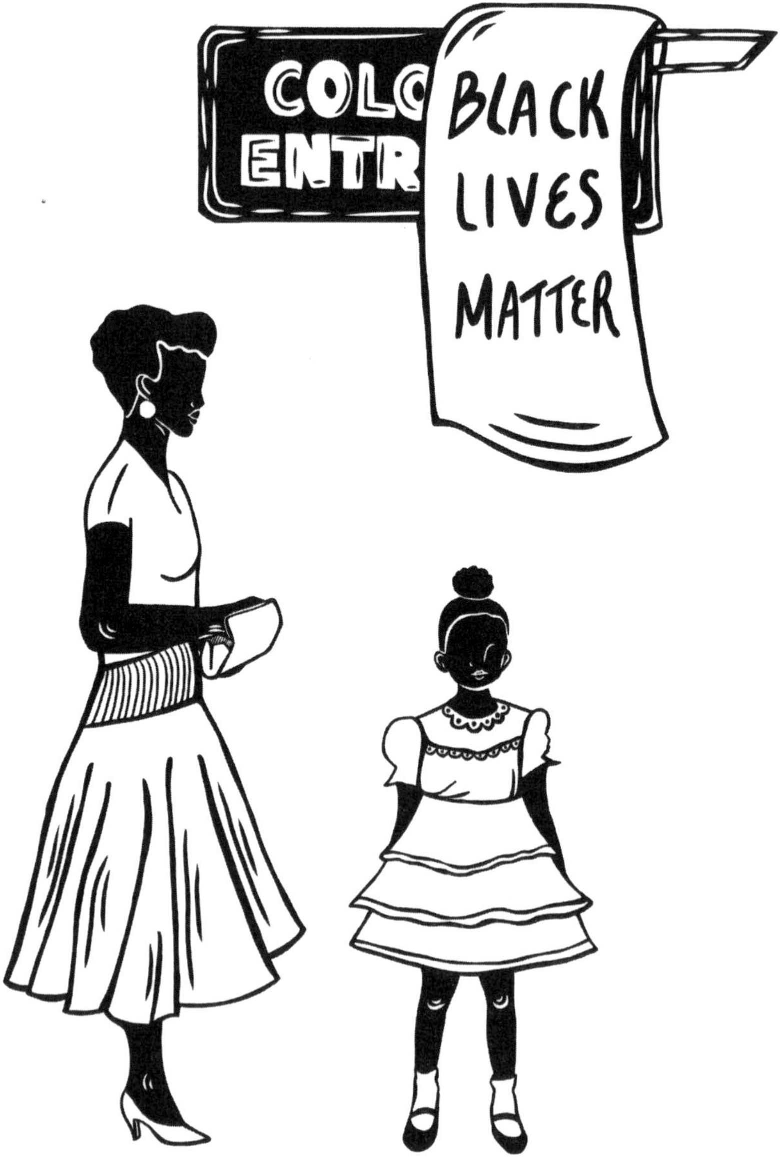
COLO
ENTR
BLACK
LIVES
MATTER

you doing time for the crime after a lifetime of limited
choices

you with your all-natural, happy-to-be-nappy Nubian 'fro

you with your perfectly coiffed Dark & Lovely flowing hair

you with skin like blackberries

you with skin like Pecan Sandies

you being the big mama, nana, grandma who's keeping
everything and everyone together

you being the big poppa, daddy, father whether the kid is
yours or not

you being the mom who's always there whether dad is
or not

you who use summer as a verb in places like Oak Bluffs
and Hilton Head

you who use summer for popsicles and open fire hydrants

you who hobnob with Jack and Jill

you who get down on Old School night

you who are following a long line of Black excellence

you who are setting a new standard for Black excellence

I see you. I know you. I know what you been through. And I know no matter what the voter suppressors/insurrectionists/haterade drinkers throw your way, you going to be alright, 'cause I got you.

Like mama cheering your team on even though the score is thirty-five to zero and there's five seconds left on the clock.

Like you're the best person on the team—even though you never left the bench.

I got you like all the play cousins and god uncles and god aunts who turn up at your kindergarten dance recital and swear the next Misty Copeland has been born.

I got you like the dad who swears this is the last time he's going to put up with your mess but still answers that midnight call.

Like the grandparents who put five dollars in your birthday cards 'cause it's all they have and you're everything they dream.

Like the way Black men greet and grab each other when it's been too long and the emotions are too strong.

Like the way the nod and a smile is all you need to know that sister has got your back—even if she doesn't know your name.

I got you like that 'cause I know that no matter your story, there is no story without you.

There is no America without Black America.

Your pain, your struggle, your joy, your success, your music, your light, your rhythm, your laughter, your love, your love, your love is the marvel of the world. Even if the world tries to tell you different.

So in those moments when the noise of negativity—from within and without—is so loud you can't hear yourself think, let yourself feel. And know without a shadow of a doubt that you are the love of my life.

Yours,
Belinda

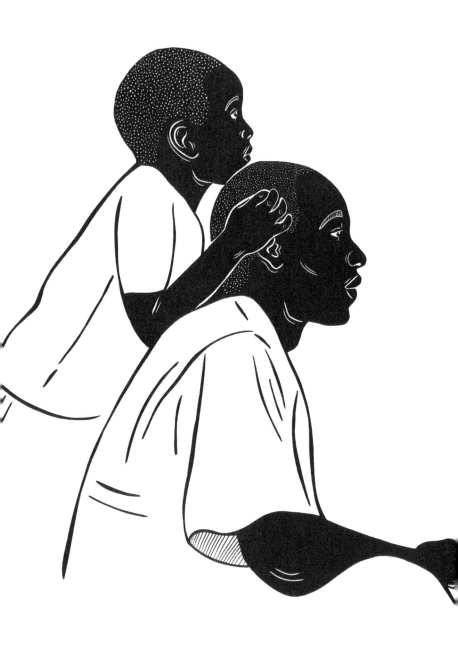

DEAR UNCLE McKINLEY

BY JONATHAN CAPEHART

All my life, you were my favorite uncle.

When I was a little kid in the 1970s, you helped provide the soundtrack of my life. Black music filled the home you shared with Aunt Annie, your childhood sweetheart. There was always R&B or soul or disco flowing from the speakers. I can still hear the crackle of the vinyl as Donna Summer sings "Last Dance" in all her disco glory.

When the grown folks were listening to the latest Richard Pryor album you picked up, replete with bad words and adult situations that didn't quite make sense to my young mind, you didn't shoo me away. You let me hang around to watch you all howl with laughter or talk back to Pryor or add your own yarn to the tale spun.

You and Aunt Annie were legends back in North Carolina. Childhood sweethearts who met when you were the high schooler driving the bus of younger kids to middle school. And your every return "back home" from the Bronx was treated like a royal visit. You were the William and Kate of that day. You delighted in family and friends as much as they delighted in you.

And when you returned to the Bronx, you taught everyone the dances you learned. I never could quite get the moves. But you encouraged me all the same.

Yours was a life filled with kindness, and the kindness you showed me at a pivotal moment in my life continues to reverberate. I was a senior in high school when I had my Carleton College interview at the New York Hilton. You were an electrician at NBC when you took my last-minute call. You let me visit you at 30 Rock knowing my fascination with the news business and NBC News in particular. You took me with you to the *Nightly News* offices, where I met a producer who would make an introduction that changed my life.

An internship at *The Today Show* with Jane Pauley and Bryant Gumbel turned into a job on *The Today Show* with Bryant Gumbel and Katie Couric. That television job oddly led me to newspapers and a Pulitzer Prize for editorial writing at the *New York Daily News.* Today, I'm an associate editor at the *Washington Post* and anchor of MSNBC's *The Sunday Show with Jonathan Capehart.*

A week before your retirement from NBC in 2012 after forty-one years, I got to bring you on at the end of *Morning Joe* to herald your career. Your humility and pride in that moment are indelibly etched in my memory. But there were two words I neglected to say to you that day that I got to say a couple days before you died in 2020: *Thank you!*

As I get older, I understand with ever more clarity how you were the quintessential good man. The kind of man who would ask, "Everything okay?" because you were the kind of person who paid attention to other people. That fateful day in the mid-1980s, you could have said no to my visit. Or you could have easily not taken the call. But that wasn't your way. You always had time. You always made time. And it is your example that will guide me always.

Love,
Your nephew, Jonathan

LOSS

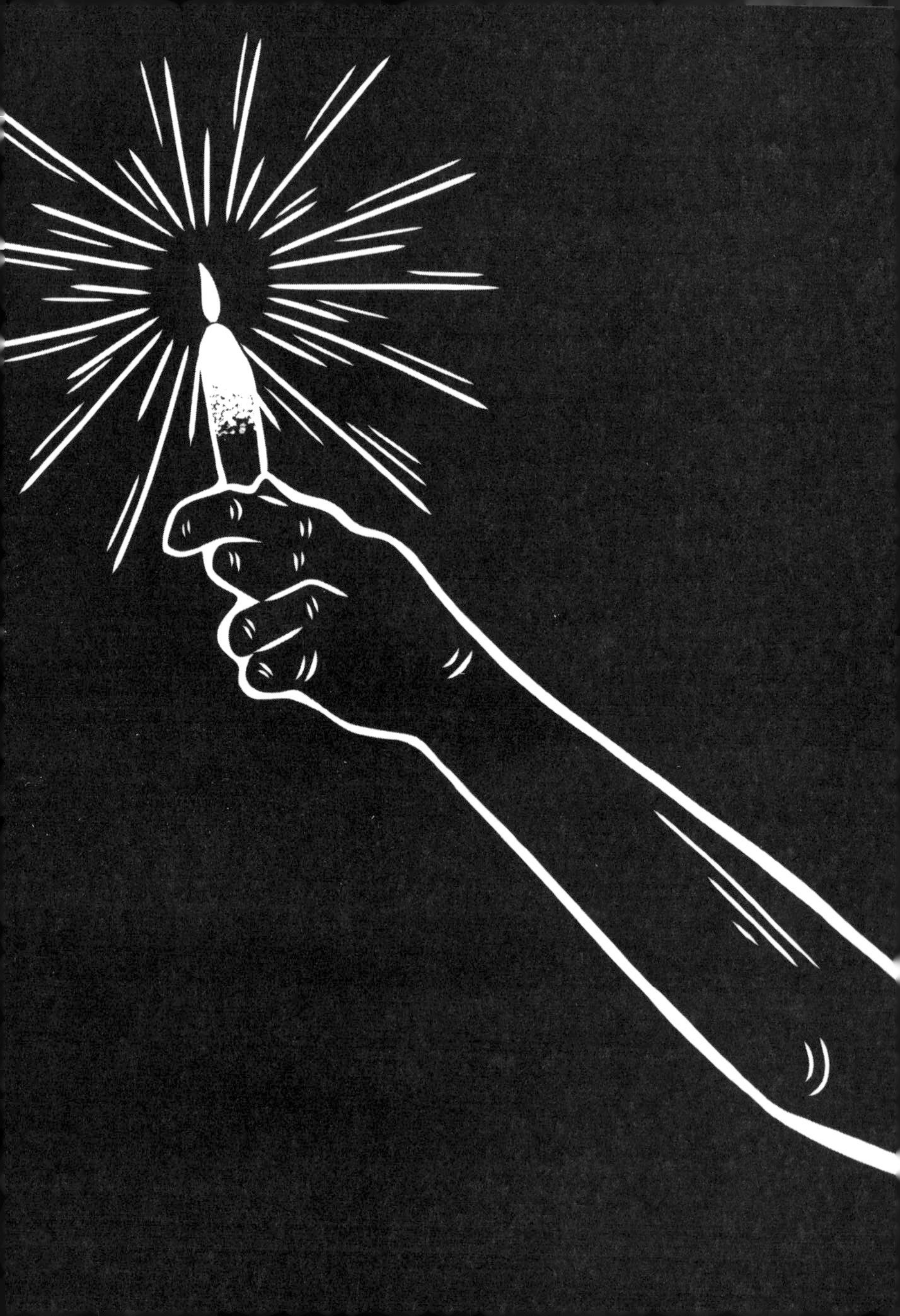

DEAR BO

BY ALLISA CHARLES-FINDLEY

Allisa's brother, Botham Jean, was murdered on September 6, 2018, when an off-duty Dallas Police Department patrol officer entered his apartment in Dallas, Texas, and fatally shot him. His name became a rallying cry for protests city- and nationwide.

BO,

I've looked at this blank page to write to you for days now. Words fail me. What can I say to you, my baby brother, my friend, my person? All I know is it has been four years, four months, and two days since I last heard your voice, since I last heard your laugh, since I last felt whole. September 6, 2018, will forever symbolize the day my world went dark. You were a light, Botham. You were the glue that held our family together. Four years, four months, two days later and we are still trying to figure out how to make it through this life without you, but because of who you were, we will do you proud.

Please forgive me for not protecting you, Botham. I play the what-if game with myself daily. What if I moved to Texas when you asked me to, what if I convinced you to move to New York, what if I encouraged you to go out with Kevin that night instead of staying home? Please forgive me. I wish I was with you to take your place that night. The world is darker without you in it.

Brandt looks more like you every day. I think he's struggling with being himself and being like you. I want him to be Brandt. You always told me, *Be you, Allisa*, and that's what I want for him. He misses you. I hate that he has been stripped of having you as a mentor. I am trying to fill that space for him, but there is only one Botham. Please look after him.

Our parents are living a daily struggle. I can tell. Dad is in denial. Four years, four months, and two days later, and he still hasn't come to terms with you being gone. He visits your grave frequently and speaks to you, sings to you. I'm sure if he closes his eyes and listens, he can hear you singing along. Mommy, on the other hand, cannot bear to visit your grave. She cannot bear knowing her son's body now resides in a cemetery. We all can't. I ask myself daily, How is this our life? How are you no longer living? How are we supposed to move on without you?

Since your untimely departure, we were left to find ways to fill the void. We created a foundation in your name to continue the great work you started in your short time on earth. The Botham Jean Foundation was created in 2018 and has since then been our way of keeping your heart beating. With every charitable deed done in your name, I see it as your heartbeat. And Botham, I want to keep your heart beating forever.

I love you, Bo. During our last conversation, we got off the phone and I forgot to tell you. I thought about calling you back but said to myself, "You will tell him next time you speak to him." That next time never came. The next time I saw you was in a casket I picked out for you. I hope you were pleased with the services we had for you. I hope we did you proud. I hope we are doing you proud.

My baby brother, visit me often in my dreams. Do not be a stranger. I feel more like Allisa when I get to speak with you in my dreams. Rest assured, we are working daily to keep your name alive and grow your legacy here on earth. It comes easy because of the angel you were. Watch over us, your family. I am looking forward to the day I get to see your face, hear your voice, and hug you for a lifetime. I miss you daily. I will love you forever. I look forward to the day we all get to meet again and live eternally with our Father in Heaven.

Until we meet again, your "Big Sis,"
Allisa

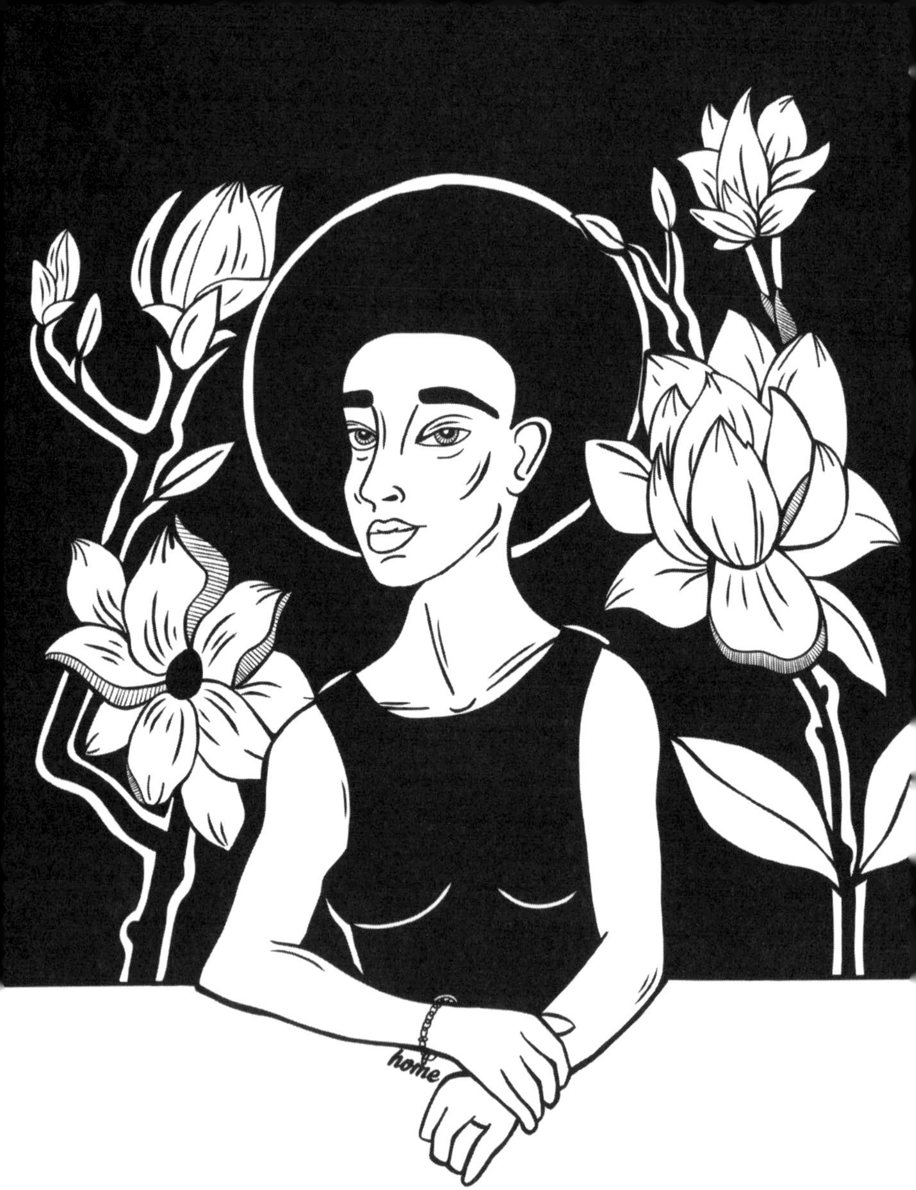
home

DEAR MOM

BY JEH CHARLES JOHNSON

Though you may be able to read and pronounce these words aloud, I know you will not be able to understand this message. Dementia has, bit by bit, year over year, robbed you of the ability to comprehend, reason, and remember. You don't know my name anymore. You can no longer grasp the concept of mother and son. You don't even know that your husband of sixty-four years and your daughter have both died.

But I look at your face and can tell that, deep in the recesses of your diminished mind, I am someone familiar to you. You still smile at me the same way you always have when I come to visit you, the same way you did on the rare occasions in my teenage years when I brought home a decent report card.

Despite your diminished capacity, you are as much my mother as the day you gave birth to me, as the days when you made me peanut butter and jelly sandwiches and took me to school, and when you loved, hugged, and doted over your grandchildren like they were your own. I still love you as I always have.

You were once an anxious person. You worried about everything. You used to constantly worry about the safety and well-being of your family. You also worried—you were even paranoid about it—that one day you would develop dementia because you knew the disease ran all throughout your family tree. About twenty-five years ago, I saw the early signs that you were slipping away. Still, one day in the early stages of the disease, you had the presence of mind to drive my wife, your daughter-in-law, to the hospital for emergency surgery. Though you have no recollection of it, you may have saved her life.

After years of anxiety and worry about all those around you, you've been granted a respite. The disease that now afflicts your mind has made you calm and at peace. I often wonder whether dementia was God's prescription for you to spare the pain you would have had to endure in your later years. You were spared the grief of your daughter's death in 2020 and your husband's death in 2021. You were oblivious as you sat in the front row of your daughter's funeral, inches away from her coffin. That night Dad died, I left the hospital to check on you, and there you were, innocently asleep in the bed you and he shared for over a half century, without a clue that he was gone forever. I considered trying to explain to you that Dad was gone. I then realized that, even if I could get you to a place where you would understand what happened, you would forget within minutes or hours. What was the point? I decided the best thing I could do was carry the grief on your behalf, along with my own.

In recent years, you've been unable to appreciate that your son, the D- student in high school, became the US secretary of homeland security. All those school years you badgered me to hunker down and study, and the values you instilled in me, finally paid dividends. Though you donated to his first campaign, you did not recognize the president when I brought you to the Oval Office. You introduced yourself to him by saying, "Hi, I'm Norma. Who are you?" He simply responded by saying, "I'm Barack. I live here." No one was embarrassed. I was glad you were there. I am glad you have lived long enough—far longer than your own mother and father—to be with me for it all.

Every day of my own sixty-five years, with you in my life, has been a gift.

Love,
Your son

DEAR GRANDMA

BY TARANA BURKE

have tried to write this letter over and over. In fact, I have written it—in my head—many, many days and nights since you left us. In the time that has passed since you've been gone, on some days, it feels like time is standing still, and on others, it feels like I am quantum leaping forward.

Reality is suspended.

The air feels different around me.

I am acutely aware that this air I breathe in is not the same air you breathe out anymore, and then I remember why, and I am folded into a pile of grief again.

Your absence is loud. And in the moments when I remember empathy, I think of the monumental losses so many of us have experienced during these tumultuous times, and the noise becomes deafening. So many of our elders were forgotten, discounted, and tossed aside in the race to solve a worldwide problem. It was lost on most that you all have more answers than we have questions. The proverb is, *Every time an elder dies, a library burns to the ground*. If that's true, then when a Black grandma dies, it's like losing ancient scrolls.

Everything I needed to survive this moment and many before now, I learned at some point from you, grandma, and I am so thankful.

You taught me to ask questions and to question everything. You were never one to settle for "no" on the first go-round. If it didn't make sense, you questioned it. If it wasn't in the best interest of your children or family, there would be questions. You had six school-aged children in four different schools and served on all the PTAs, and when I asked you why, you said, "Because no one will be making decisions about my kids without me!" I can just imagine you in those meetings raising your hand and asking more questions than they thought a "colored" woman should. You were an early example to me that there is usually another answer if you are willing to ask questions.

You taught me fortitude. The definition of this word includes phrases like "moral strength," "firmness of purpose," and "strength of mind," to name a few. These are all things that you not only exemplified but made sure we knew were key ingredients to being a good person. And I really spent time dissecting what made you such a good person to me, Grandma, because you weren't particularly preachy, and you didn't waste your time pontificating. You lived your goodness with an ease that allowed people to experience it however they experienced you.

You didn't put a lot of words on paper, but you helped me build an emotional and spiritual canon. It has been invaluable.

This is why I wanted to write to you, Grandma. Your life and your loss will never be taken for granted. Every memory, lesson, and experience is value added to my life. Every day of your nine decades mattered. And I will never take for granted what it meant for you to always show up for me—for us all. And you did, Grandma. You were able to teach me so much because you were ever present in my life—in all our lives. You showed up when I needed you and when I didn't know I needed you.

You lived through nine decades of struggle. Segregation and migration. Depression and suppression. Hard choices and the fight to choose. And you always stood on the right side of history. You deserved more than what this country was willing to give you in the end, Grandma. All of you did. But if it means anything, I will always stand up for you. I will always be grateful for you. I will always represent you and do everything in my power to make you proud.

My goal in life is to be a library for someone else like you were for me, Grandma. I hope I make you proud.

I love you,
Tarana

NAMESAKE

BY NATALIE JOHNSON

I can't braid my hair like you could. The dexterity and patience necessary never came naturally to me, especially considering my relationship with hair growing up. Black hair was the cause of a never-ending family melodrama. Curls turned into knots, knots turned into tangled masses, and tangled masses turned into my grandmother's tears. "The child's hair!" she'd cry out in defeat at the bird's nest that had formed in her absence.

But in you stepped. Aunt Marge. Knots, tangles, tears—you didn't mind. You would gently dip my head in a plastic bowl of warm water like a religionless baptism and patiently work away. We spent many sweaty August evenings with my head resting in your lap while you combed and twisted well past midnight. Johnson women were blessed with strong arms, you told me, and those arms absorbed every oncoming yank, so I'd never have to wince in pain.

You were tender and giving with everyone but yourself.

It was in those late hours I realized you were the brightest person I knew. You brought me into the fold of Black feminist

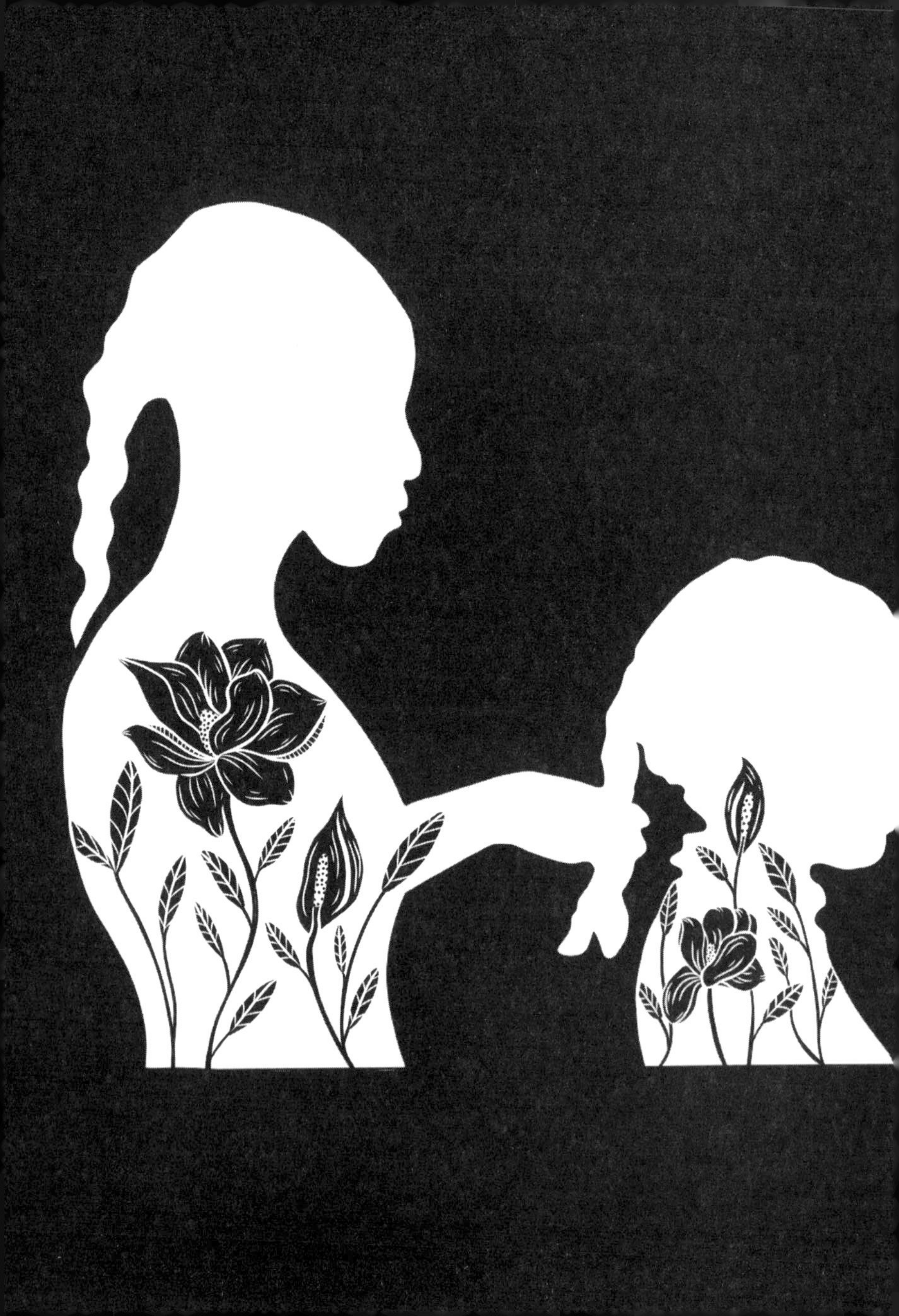

thinkers with Toni Morrison, Zora Neale Hurston, and your namesake, Miss Marguerite Johnson, who the world knew as Maya Angelou. Together we probed life's biggest questions: Why are we here? And what does it mean to live a meaningful life?

I wish you had chosen to live your life. I wish you would have embraced even the most broken bits so that you might still be with us. If someone told me I could have absorbed your pain in my arms as you did mine, I would have certainly tried.

You died on February 26, 2020. Ash Wednesday. I drove from New York City with your brother to the hospital room you lay in. I held his hand. How painful it must be to serve as the bookend of your baby sister's life when you did everything to save her. My mom waited for us at the foot of your bed, her forehead marked with a charcoal cross. None of us are particularly religious, but it was a small piece of poetry for the moment. All life comes to an end, and we return to the dust from which we came.

The old adage is that we should never speak ill of the dead. But to memorialize a person's life as they lived is a complicated task. Many things can be true at once. Marguerite was kind. Marguerite was brilliant. Marguerite liked Disney movies and sewed us Christmas stockings by hand. Marguerite loved me and Jeh like the kids she never had. Marguerite made us feel seen. Marguerite was beautiful. Marguerite gave away more than she kept. Marguerite had two poisonous marriages. Marguerite was an alcoholic. Marguerite was struggling. Marguerite could not let the past go. Marguerite died of liver failure, and she died too young. Marguerite was my namesake. Marguerite belonged to me. I belong to her.

I may always feel a tightness in my chest whenever I hear "Birmingham" mentioned in a sentence or when my dad says he sees your face in mine. It's difficult to make peace with how much of our lives you will miss.

There's a silhouette of your profile Granddad paid a local artist to draw when you were a girl. It's an outline of a little nose, forehead, and braid falling down your back. *Marguerite was here*, it says to me. The paper has begun to brown, and the edges have begun to fray, but your imprint—on the page, on us, on me—that is forever.

I understand now that love is imperfect, but it is always within reach. We can choose it even in our most painful hour. And because you couldn't love your broken bits, I will love them for you. I will love them with the same force that loves the sound of your voice and the kindness of your heart. And when I have a little girl resting her head in my lap, I will tell them who Marguerite Johnson was. Marguerite was here. Marguerite was loved.

Your namesake,
Natalie Marguerite Johnson

DEAR DAD

BY BILL WHITAKER

You never told me things would become clearer with age.

As a youngster, I loved and respected you as my father, the authority figure in the house. The older I grow, the more I respect you as a man; the more I appreciate the love you wrapped around us like a security blanket; the more I understand the sacrifices you made for your family.

To be clear, you were a task master. You grew up in the South where "children should be seen, not heard" and "spare the rod, spoil the child" were not *just* proverbs but seem lifted straight from some old-school child-rearing manual that Black adults seemed to know by heart. Fortunately for my sisters and me, aside from the occasional spanking (we called them whoopings), the old-school rules were leavened by your migration north. For us, it was distilled down to "respect and honor your mother and father."

And we did.

We shared so many memories, Dad. I remember you taking me at five to get my hair cut on Olive St., teaching me to ride a two-wheel bike in front of the house and sitting with us in the pew at church. There was the time you took me to a Phillies game

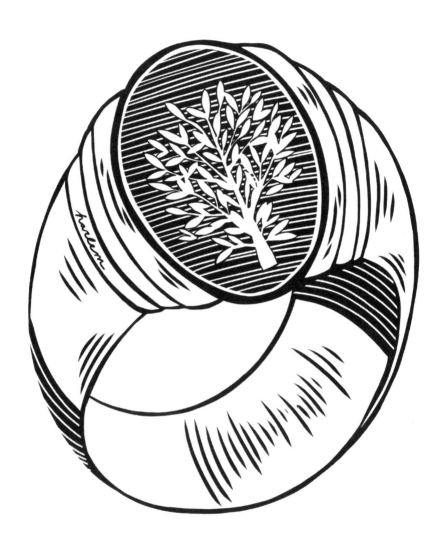

with my Cub Scout troop, even though you hated the Phillies because of the way their manager, Ben Chapman, harassed Jackie Robinson twenty years earlier.

You were a proud Black man, passionate about improving the lot of Black people. I remember you went with the local NAACP to the March on Washington in 1963, and when you got home, you told us Martin Luther King Jr. was your candidate for orator of the century.

I remember you would leave early in the morning to go to work as a welder at the shipyard. It was hard, gritty work. Mom would drive to pick you up after your shift, and often I'd tag along. When the whistle blew, thousands of men would pour off the docks and out of the warehouses. I'd spot you in the throng and jump out of the car and run to greet you. You'd lift me up and carry me back to the car. (That memory still warms me today.) And when you got home, you'd take a shower and sit down in front of the TV to watch the news; we kids had to be quiet while you caught up on the important events of the day. That was your evening ritual—ours, actually, because I'd watch with you. I think that's where I caught the news bug.

There were so many memories we created together but many more we weren't able to share. Like too many Black men, you died way too soon—a series of strokes took you from us when you were sixty-five and I was thirteen. I remember people saying what a horrible age to lose your father, as though there's a good age. But you should know you had already left such an imprint on me. I had a path to follow, a role model to emulate. You were proud without being prideful, you worked hard without complaining, and you cared for your family through good times and bad. That was the foundation you laid for me.

I've learned much more about you in the decades since you passed away.

I know you fled the tobacco fields of eastern North Carolina during the Great Migration, drawn to the hustle and bustle of 1920s Harlem. You worked as a waiter at the Cotton Club, that famed Harlem nightspot where Duke and Ella performed—but also where white patrons came in the front door while the Black staff and entertainers came in the back.

I know you dreamed of being a journalist, and I've since come across some of the articles and opinion pieces you wrote for the now defunct *Harlem Bulletin*. But you knew, a Black man making a living as a journalist at that time was little more than a pipe dream. So, when you and Mom started a family, you put down your pen and picked up a welding torch. You left the excitement of Harlem for small-town Pennsylvania so we kids could attend good schools. Your New York family laughed that you'd become a country bumpkin, but you did it for us. Education was vitally important to you; our house was full of books. You'd be proud to know all three of your children graduated from college and have advanced degrees—not a bad legacy for a self-taught man whose formal education ended at eighth grade.

When I went off to college, Mom gave me the ring you wore all your adult life. It is simple and strong, a black onyx oval set in a gold band. I've been wearing this ring all my adult life, and it has been all over the world with me in my career as a broadcast journalist. It has been to almost sixty countries and has shaken hands with presidents, celebrities, and some of the most astounding people whose names so often go unsung.

When I got the job as correspondent for *60 Minutes*, my family and I moved from Los Angeles to New York and settled in Harlem. One day, walking through the streets of my new neighborhood, it hit me—this ring had been here before; it had walked these streets and seen these sights . . . with you.

So many things have become clearer with age. My own life has an arc I could not have imagined. And this ring, I now see it as more than a cherished memento—it is connective tissue that binds our lives together. I'm a journalist, living in Harlem. In so many ways, I'm living the life you had dreamed of living.

I have been fortunate to see my children grow into adults and begin to create their own arcs. I wish you could have been around to see the family tree that has grown from the seeds you planted. I would love for you to know your legacy lives on. I think you'd be proud.

Your son,
Bill

ANCESTORS

BY JUSTUS CORNELIUS PUGH

To Papa Dell,   Nanni Violet,   Granny Doris,
Granny,   T-Shirley,   Gran-Daddy,   Aunt MaryAnne,
and Papa, my namesake.

I love you, I miss you,
                and I wish we got more time.

Saying sunrise and sunset instead of life and death
doesn't make losing y'all any easier,
            but it does help the vibrancy and light of your life
            shine through the dull clouds of your passing.

And the more I thought of you with every passing
                    dawn and dusk,
                            the more you became a part of it.

There are days that pass
when I wish I could go back to

watching old westerns by your bedside,

    or

watching the guaranteed surprise in your faces when
you saw how big I've gotten

    or

watching you deal cards and comebacks while stacking
books and bills

    or

watching you tend to cucumbers and tomatoes and roses
    before telling me to get to work too.

And now you watch me,

from above,

extending like smoke from my altar,

    crowning me like a halo.

    You're with me.

Tag teaming with High John the Conqueror

    and a bag of crystals,

    harmonizing in messages delivered through meditation.

    You're with me.

When I rub shea butter on my body

and when I forgot my feet the other day
and subconsciously let out a "sorry,"
I knew that

you're with me.

It's been easier to take care of myself
when I do it in y'all's honor.
It becomes less of a chore and more of a responsibility.

You're teaching me devotion
and self-love and   I'm learning how many selves
                                     there are to love and the depth
                                     of all that's reflected in my own.

And in those reflections, you reveal parts of yourselves that
unlock the deepest parts of me.

        While I wish we got more time,
        I wonder if I would have learned all of this if you were
        still here.

Often, people think that I write stories and poems to
share things I've learned,
but in the act of writing is where the learning happens.
When I put pen to the page,   it feels like conversation.

Like I'm opening up the
path for your messages to
flow to me.

A loved one told me that

"Your ancestors might be communicating with you
internally through writing and meditation, but they
may also be communicating with you through people
you commune with."

And another said,

"When our ancestors pass,
in a lot of ways, we get closer.
We aren't limited to words when we communicate
with them,
but they can feel what we feel and see what we see,
and there's nothing between them and us anymore,
nothing that can get lost in translation."

And I sum all this up to ubiquity.
Presence

within every heartbeat,
        yet holding both my hands,
                while lifting me up   on your shoulders,
                        and still watching over me from above.

Wrapping up lessons in the shape of coincidences.
Gifting me your dreams in the form of my imagination.
Using nature as an envoy for messages I expect the least
and need the most.

Taking all my hopes and worries
and tossing them in the sky　　to dance in red and purple hues,
reminding me to
take an inhale and exhale out
I love you
and àse.

To my elders,
my ancestors,
my ascendants.

HEY DAD

BY RHIANNA JONES

How's life treating you up there? I miss you, but I feel you in the blue jays and butterflies dancing in the air. Hugging me each morning through the sun's warm embrace, the same sun we watched rise and fall from your bedside on the lake. If only I'd known that our journey of bonding and learning would become my path of wondering and yearning. If only I'd known.

I remember it like yesterday. Clutching your cold, limp hand, the fear mounting in your eyes as you took your last few breaths. Mom beside you, holding you gently to ease you back to rest. Me calling hospice madly to calm your hyperventilating chest. Then it stopped. Your breath stopped. Your heart stopped. Time stopped. I screamed so loud her car swerved on the other end of the call. My tears cascaded over your lifeless body like Niagara Falls. My fighter, your four-year battle may have come to a close, but the throes of a Black Revolution had yet to show. My father, Tyrone Xavier Jones, if only you'd known the fire and fury that were growing in our bones.

Have you met George Floyd? Breonna Taylor? Ahmaud Arbery? Or any who lifted the complacency cocoon with their stolen pleads? An agonizing summer almost normalizing the Black loss flooding our feeds. You left too soon, but your last breath was not a protest, hashtag, nor live stream. It feels almost a privilege for Blacks to have a private death in peace. I wish you'd held on a little longer. As my only Black family, enduring BLM without you made my curiosity grow fonder. So many unanswered questions, Daddy. If only I'd known.

I wish I knew you as a young boy. You said you wanted to be remembered for bringing others laughter and joy. Indeed, you left a mile of smiles in your wake. You even left this earth with a smile upon your face. A glimmer of the gummy smile you gave me that lights up every room and space. While you've left a hole in my heart that can never be replaced, know at my core that I am happy, and I am safe. Grateful for the last weeks we spent together, healing our wounds, saying all there was to say. The hardest was watching you call each and every friend through sadness and pain. Reminiscing one last time before your body washed away. Of your profound love and loyalty for them, I'll forever be amazed. In writing this, I remember how grief's surreality comes and goes in waves. As your only child and daughter, Tyrone Xavier Jones, I miss you deeply as I navigate my life's many milestones.

Thank you for leaving an archive behind for me to explore. Discovering your life through your curated treasures, being uniquely Rhi was your gift all the more. We always joked we shared nothing in common beyond DNA, but know that now, our synergy deepens day by day. To our similitude, my gratitude: For your unending courage, as the only inner-city Black kid to graduate your suburban white enrichment school. With all their hate and fear you swallowed, alone, far from home, finding your way, and Mom is pretty fucking cool. For your beaming confidence, moving solo to New York for MFA but truly to pursue stand-up as Pryor's protégé. For your magnetic energy, whether finessing yourself through Studio 54 or commanding any room upon walking through the door. For your intellectual curiosity, a walking encyclopedia of Black sports, politics, and history, you should've been the sportscaster dissecting playbacks on the screen. So much light exuding from one being, but sadly, society and the system hindered you from living out your dreams. You even abbreviated your clearly Black name for more chances to succeed. So much more I would wish for you. If only I'd known.

And in my learning journey I've come to see, the many nuances and privileges of my biraciality. Thank you for the greatest gift of all. The honor of the culture I get to call, my people, my power, my kin. BLACK. From my Afro curls, and truth-dropping lips, to my sista girls, and beat-bopping hips. Oh how I LOVE my melanin. Thank you for raising me on Miles Davis, Donna Summer, and Al Green. As dancing was our happy place, I wrote your LETTER with musicality. Despite being historically stripped, our culture's so abundant and rich—in community, care, and creativity. I followed your path from Harlem to Brooklyn to immerse myself where our culture spills onto the streets. I chose this for my personal reeducation, to undo decades of Eurocentric conditioning and colonization. But every day the faces and families change as gentrification engulfs this nation like a plague. My friend called me the Beyoncé of Bed-Stuy—fitting, as the first concert you took me to was Destiny's Child. I may not have her platform or power, but you taught me to never silence my voice nor cower. So as I continue my journey learning how *Black Is King*, I strive to spread smiles and sunshine energy. I may not reach global legendry, but if I can brighten this planet and the people whose lives I grace, I know I'd make you proud, with that gummy smile upon your face.

I wish you could see the incredible woman I've come to be. Know with heart and soul I promise to build our legacy. While your story didn't meet your revered Barack's and Jordan's glory, you're my hero. And now, the world will finally know . . . the magic of Tyrone Xavier Jones.

Your only,
Rhianna Jones

DEAR DAD

BY DOUG JONES

I feel robbed.

We only started our friendship back when I moved into the downstairs apartment for graduate school. Do you remember what you said to me after you said I could live there? "If ever the traffic through the apartment gets uncomfortable for me and your mother, we will ask you to leave." Took my breath away. At twenty-eight, I wondered who you thought I'd become. I was the person you had raised. I was every bit of who you had declared, demanded, pleaded, begged, prayed, forced, cajoled, coerced, and strong-armed me into becoming. And in one breathtaking moment, all of that had been reduced to "traffic," such being your euphemistic way of saying you didn't want to see, hear, or encounter any aspect of my gay "lifestyle." I did everything I could to not move back into that brownstone with you and Ma. But Columbia was unyielding about not extending housing to students who had family living within a fifty-mile radius of NYC. And even back in 1996, NYC rent wasn't cheap—especially coupled with grad school tuition. That Bed-Stuy garden apartment in the house where I grew up was a gift and a curse. We were

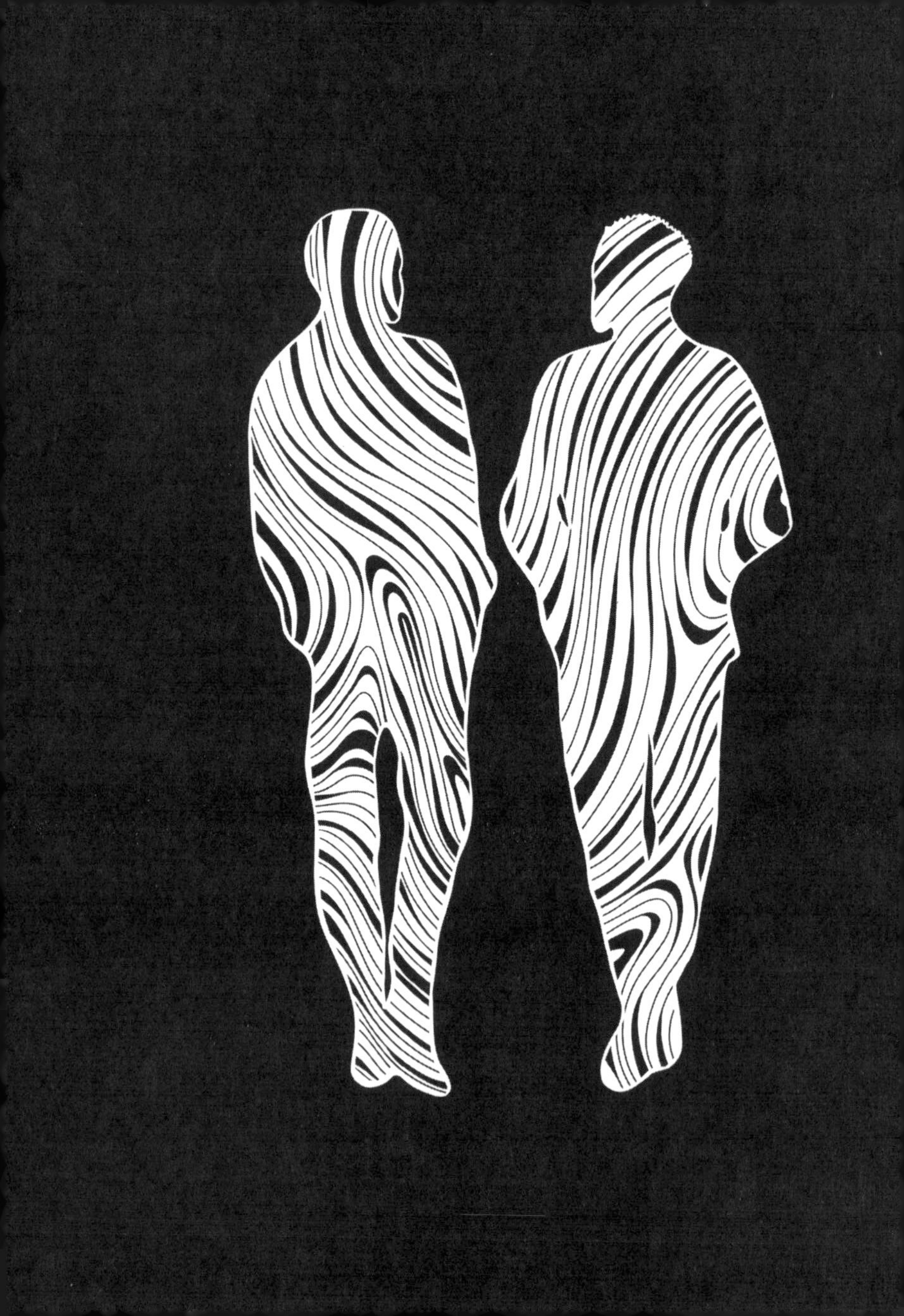

father and son, and there was love, but we had never really *liked* each other, Dad, did we? Not like you and Duane. Not like me and Ma. Well. God would show us, wouldn't He? And He certainly did.

Even with living in the ground-floor garden apartment, those first few months, things were so tentative. For my part, I tried not to breathe too loudly. Music low, TV quiet, careful about visitors. Weekend meals every so often with you and Ma helped locate neutral territory. You wanted to hear about school, especially when I took that class with Michael Eric Dyson. I would tell you that Columbia was different from Morehouse in every way imaginable. I couldn't have attended undergraduate school at Columbia; emotionally, psychologically, I wouldn't have survived. Racist overtones and intonations haunted everything. The presence of non-white bodies there was a necessary accommodation only to be tolerated until someone thought of something better. Remember our long conversation about Black writing and the dominance of Morrison, Walker, and McMillan on the bestseller lists at that time? I wanted to know where our modern equivalent was. Where was our current-day Baldwin, Wright, and Hughes? "He's at the tip of your pen." Here we are decades later, and your response still lights my insides.

Slowly, surely, and with the certainty of the Divine, God transformed us right before our eyes. I finished Columbia in two years. Shortly after graduation and before I moved out to my apartment, Ma told me, "Your father is having such a *fantastic* time with you!" Dad, we had become *friends*. We talked about everything, most especially work stuff related to me navigating the New York political world of economic development but also about the changing landscape of Bed-Stuy; the rising cost of real estate (when was I going to buy a house?!); my frustrating trials with the New York publishing world; my relationship with my brother and his relationship with our future daughter/ sister-in-law; and, every once in a very, very, very blue moon, the open secret of my romantic life. My relationship with Chadra was not what you and Ma hoped for, but I'm still thrilled she's become a very treasured part of our family. I think we all are. I was humbled when you invited my closest friends over for a night of drinks and hors d'oeuvres, even while saying you didn't want to know anything of "the affair" you correctly guessed I was having with one of them. You had become my guide and con- fidant, my usher and my touchstone. I consulted with you about everything, from what career moves I should make to seeking your advice about the brownstone I'd eventually buy. You reminded me to give myself grace in the development of my writ- ing: "Something like that takes years of experience. Look at Morrison." And you always kept it real—ever attentive to my tales of frustration with my very demanding boss at Hunter College, you typically agreed with her—a *compassionate Republican*, of all things!

None of us—not Ma, Duane, me, any of your brothers nor your sister, none of your nieces or nephews, not one of your friends, no one—were prepared when you were diagnosed with Parkinson's. It has been five years now, and the sight of your six-foot-three, three-hundred-plus-pound frame reduced to a shrinking mass of clothes and blankets sitting stationary in a wheelchair in front of a television is maddening. When I think about the man you are—the patriarch of our family; the husband you are; the father you are; the grandfather you are; the children you have raised; the houses you purchased and renovated (for our family, for me, for my brother); the debt-free undergraduate education you provided for me and my brother; your charity; the friends and community you support, it just seems so cruel. Unduly so. Unnecessarily so. To never walk with you again. To never see you drive again. To never again hear you speak a coherent sentence. That you will always require round-the-clock home-care assistance. To not be able to see your eyes mirror my excitement at the news that finally—*finally!*—my long-anticipated dream of being published will come true when Simon & Schuster publishes my novel in 2024. To not be able to let you know that after many romantic twists and turns, I'm doing okay—it's still early, but that affair you referenced two decades ago might just blossom into something incredible. Parkinson's has muted me in fear, shame, guilt, and anger. Parkinson's has been a specter hovering over my therapy sessions. Remarkably, your Parkinson's diagnosis has been a cauldron of emotions helping me evolve.

Dad, I opened this letter saying that I felt robbed. As the disease has progressed, I thought limiting our interaction would reduce the hurt—out of sight, out of mind. It has only made the memory of you ache that much more. And the true cruelty is to continue to allow this disease to rob us of these moments. This heist, this piracy of our relationship necessitates a clarity of perception in order to repossess who we are to one another. I understand you to be a complex man of highly evolved morals, ethics, and way of being, all of which you imparted to me as your son. Some of those values have conformed to my understanding of myself. Others have had to be recalibrated to fit my definition of myself as a Black gay man. Parkinson's attempted theft has replaced the solid foundation afforded by certain confirmation with the loving flexibility afforded by the fluid divinity of grace: I know you are as proud of me, as the son you made me to be, as I am of you, the patriarch and father who made me.

I love you.

Your Son,
Doug

TO ERIKA

BY MAHOGANY BROWNE

DEAR ERIKA,

I don't come to you with open arms, just this one hand, palm outreached. But I have come to this side of the bridge in hopes that you can find your way to the other side of the same infrastructure, with a desire to meet me in the middle of the road too.

Over a decade ago, in our final hours of active sistering, I believe we both didn't show up as our best selves. I can only imagine what Grandma Coco would say if she saw us tussle words, purses, and hands until only shreds of our already tattered relationship remained dying into a pool of silence between us. She never liked us to argue. And honestly, I despise arguing too. But like all things we hate, we become frighteningly good at the thing that curdles our blood. So one might look at our family time together as destructive. The way you called me Bitch when we played dominoes and I won. The way I made fun of your clothes (the same clothes I would hope to wear one day when you forget them on the floor of your closet) all a special formula that made up our dialect of love.

And we were taught unconditional love. It was you that encouraged me to forgive our mother for the stolen childhood. And it was you who called me whenever you needed me to *mollywop* someone for disrespecting you. And this is the thing that made me feel most seen by you. It made duty feel like affection. This is also why I stopped fighting the day we stopped speaking.

We were taught: "That's your blood. That's you family. That's all you got." From Louisiana and Texas to Cali. From slavery mentality to the tremors of post trauma slave syndrome. But it was New York that gave me space and clarity to understand that the kind of love we were taught wasn't necessarily the kind of love that sustains. It got us this far, but the model was broken and lopsided. It didn't allow love to be in conversation with accountability, and we suffered so many needless family gatherings without one another for its inability to satiate our desires to feel like whole individuals.

It was in New York, sister, that I realized unconditional love should not be a knee-jerk reaction that you are born into, but an obligation you wake gladly to each day. Sister love is a thing that keeps me hopeful. It is how I carved this life into something that I can hold. It has picked me up from the ground during heartbreak, and delivered soup to my home when illness was the only song I owned. Sisterships are most important to me because they serve as my barometer for who I am in the world. I am only here because of you, dear sister. Everything I write is a song to keep your attention.

You were not always cruel. You were once the only daughter of our mother, whose heart was so broken she couldn't see the ways in which we chipped away at each other all those years. You are my first heartbreak, sister. I couldn't see you clearly then, not the way I see you now. You were scared. You were angry. And when I was born—you felt replaced? abandoned? dismissed? But you were always who I tried to impress. My adoration for you grew louder in hopes of absorbing your annoyance. So I pray you can accept this letter as a request for a new kind of love for us. A love that can carry both our bruised inner children in its warm orb, a place where we can both heal and grow together. It is true, we haven't had the best models of good sister love. TV don't count, right?

Toni Morrison wrote, "Love is or it ain't. Thin love ain't love at all," and one might think this is the mantra to consider when diving into the romantic waters. But I grew into a woman, using this quote to understand our love. When I awakened my artistic self and I asked you to respect the name of my choosing. It was thin love that refused me. When I invited you to the opening of my first one-woman show and you countered the invitation with a glowing review of the choreographer, never once noting the poems I wrote about our mother's survival. It was thin love that refused me. And I know you know love. Grandma Coco taught us through examples as she returned to her church every Sunday service. And you proved it was possible at my lowest moments: when I was low on rent during my first couple of years in New

York City. But we both deserve a profound, earthly, growing, and soaring kind of love story. One for sisters who protect each other from the world.

Take my hand, Erika. Let Grandma Coco's prayers lead us forward.

Your devoted little sis,

M

IV

AMBIVALENCE

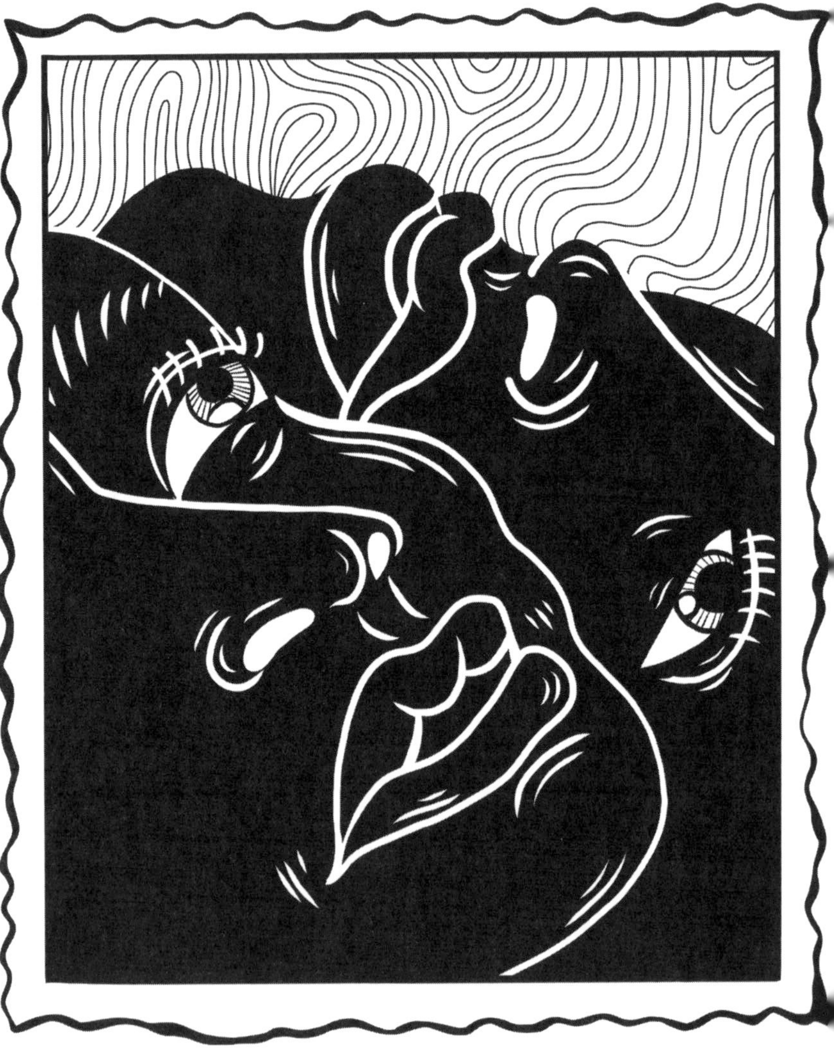

WORRY

BY TOPAZ JONES

I worry.

Fingers running through coarse curls
Obsessively detangling
Constantly caught at the root of my deepest insecurity

You've yet to be conditioned

What song will you sing?
What words will rest sweetly against your mother tongue?
We'll do our best to weave strands of your past
Together
But will they hold?

I worry.

Perhaps I can't love you enough

To offset the contempt I keep for myself
The soles of your ballet flats will have worn smooth before
you've ever tried
them on

I worry.

> One day you'll lose
> your footing

And stop dancing altogether
Scratching your head
Resisting the urge
To middle part your existence

I worry.

> You'll favor your
> mother

And although her yellow skin and high cheekbones will make
you desirable to
many I'll only be able to see the presumptions of onlookers
And deciding what movie to watch or where to eat dinner will
feel like a referendum

And I will have unwittingly drawn a circle
Returning to the dawn of your grandmother's dissonant
upbringing

Like a refrain in a rhyme I thought I was freestyling

That when I do sit down to write

        I will be fearful

And the blank slate of an empty page will mock me
And my shame will reverberate across the hall
And your twists will begin to unravel

I'm worried.

        I too was once a tender-headed child

Created in response to grief
Received for the first time as if returning from a lengthy,
tumultuous journey
More heirloom than heir
Large, glossy eyes gazing upward

        A mirror

Reflecting an assemblage of funny, familiar faces
Mouths agape, stomachs in knots, sleeves stained with salt
water, still.
They know of the delicate balance
The fine, fragile material used to sew generations of ambitions
and fears, traumas
and triumphs
The breath, conservatively held in anticipation of having to
expel it all

And never being able to explain it all

I will be staring down with them when you arrive
Savoring the wonderment of a miracle performed
And just like them

I'll worry.

MARCUS AL SHARPTON BRIGHT

BY REVEREND AL SHARPTON

I remember so well getting the call that you had arrived almost four years ago. Your mother, Dominique, gave birth to you in a hospital on the West Side, and I rushed to see you. When I got there, a nurse asked me if I wanted to hold my grandson—a question I was damn certain I would never hear. They placed you in my arms, and I felt overcome with emotion. I've never experienced a moment so surreal.

You see, in my line of work, another day was never guaranteed. I stepped into the tradition of civil rights leaders—race men. Fighting for equality for our people—all people—became my life's work. I was raised by men you'll read about one day— John Lewis, Jesse Jackson. They taught me how to organize, how to press truth to power. But we never discussed retirement plans. They didn't bother teaching me how to age. Our leaders had short life expectancies in those days.

My mentors were raised by a generation of race men that never got old. You'll soon know their names: Martin Luther King Jr., Medgar Evers, Malcolm X. None of them made it to forty. Bobby and John Kennedy barely did. Even if we didn't talk about it—John, Jesse, and I—we all assumed we would meet the same end. Assassination was an occupational hazard for folks on the frontlines of the struggle. We knew what we risked each day.

In the winter of 1991, my visions nearly became reality. I was preparing to lead a march in Bensonhurst, New York, when a young man walked up to me calmly and stuck a steak knife in my chest. The blade missed my heart by an inch. If he had had his way, neither you nor I would exist today.

I fell to the ground, and the partners gathered around me leapt into action. I swear to you, Marcus, despite all the chaos, during those moments when I lay on the ground, blood pooling around me, I felt peace. I had dedicated myself to a cause and neared the end that I knew might one day come. I had no regrets. I'd served my purpose.

One day, you'll learn about the work your grandfather did. On that same day, people might try to convince you to despair. They might tell you that, despite our efforts, nothing changed because nothing *ever* changes.

Do not believe them.

I marched for Mandela's freedom, and I watched from Johannesburg when he won the presidency. I was born into an

America that laughed at the thought of a Black president, and I sat nearby on Barack Obama's inauguration day. You'll mature in a world where the possibility of a Black man running this country is a foregone conclusion. For you, his presidency is history.

Our lineage is a testament to our progress. Neither of my parents, your great-grandparents, finished elementary school. They grew up in the Jim Crow South, attending segregated schools, and when it was time to go to work, they went. I got a shot at college. Your mother graduated from Temple University. In two generations, our family went from illiteracy to college graduates. We never buckled under the weight of oppression. We kept striving.

You come from a bloodline that was repressed, suppressed, and oppressed but never broken. Don't ever let anyone tell you that our struggle didn't bear fruit. Those fools don't know how bad it was. You're living proof of progress.

Marcus Al Sharpton Bright, you carry a name that I thought would end with me. I am in you. Everything I have done since you arrived has been to hand you a name that you can feel proud of, a legacy that you can reach for.

You must know that you have a responsibility too. It is your duty to struggle as we did. I don't expect you to become a civil rights leader. I don't *want* you to become a civil rights leader. But I do expect you to struggle; you must advance the cause of equality in whatever way suits you. You must be at least as determined to strive as they are to keep you down. The Movement is your inheritance. Accept it and do a little more for the ones that come after you. That's all I can ever ask.

Love,
Papa Al

TO MY TWENTY-YEAR SELF-LOVE JOURNEY

BY BRIANNA HOLT

Like many Black women, I spent the majority of my youth being taught that there was something wrong with my expression, my existence, my being. But I think my greatest struggle as a child was falling in love with myself, with the way my hair defies gravity, with the way my lips protrude from my face, and with the way the sun kisses my skin.

At an early age, I learned to hate every part of my being that made me unique. In elementary school, I was first told that my hair was nappy. I remember begging my mom to let me get a relaxer so I "could have straight hair like the white girls," and a few years later, she finally caved. Although my kinky coils were now straight as a line, it didn't change my experience, at least not to the extent I had hoped. Instead of fitting in with the white girls, I was no longer teased about my hair, which as a result of the relaxer became extremely dry, thin, and brittle.

In middle school, I was first told that my lips were too big, so I swore that I would never wear lipstick or lip gloss because I

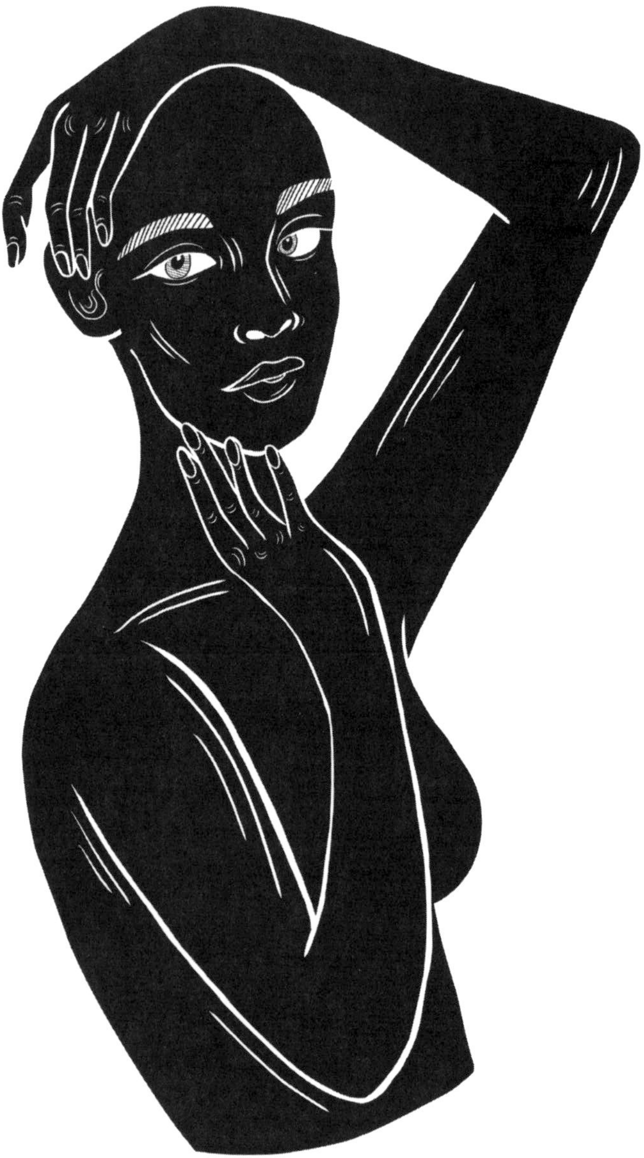

didn't want to draw attention to my large pout. I once went so far as to Google "lip reduction" surgery. Luckily, I was instantly disturbed by the YouTube videos that showed full lips being cut in half with a scalpel to remove fat. I could never put myself through anything that major.

In high school, I was constantly made aware of the distaste some people held for my dark skin tone. When it came to my skin, I felt hopeless. It covered my entire body. It was the one thing I couldn't really change or hide. After experimenting with lightening creams and avoiding the sun, I gave up and decided that I would have to live with being ugly forever.

Finally, in college, something changed. A guy called my skin smooth, flawless, and beautiful. I couldn't understand it. Surely he must be joking or just trying to be nice. But he was right. My skin *was* smooth, as smooth as a baby's bottom. My skin was flawless, free from breakouts or damage by the sun. And most of all, my chocolate skin glistened in the sun, presenting a rich tone that felt warm. Of course, my skin was beautiful. After all, it's black. That same year, I was motivated by Black girlfriends to transition my hair back to its natural state. We were tired of suffering from the damage relaxers had put our hair through. It was also during college when I would first overhear mostly white women complaining in public bathroom mirrors about having thin lips and wishing they could get lip fillers. It was as if everything I had been ridiculed for and taught to hate during my adolescence was now socially acceptable, and even more, sought after.

It saddens me that it took nearly twenty years for me to not only appreciate but *love* the skin I'm in, the locks that grow from my scalp, and the full lips that I have naturally. How could I, a Black woman, ever believe that my features, the same features that quite literally bolster the cosmetic industry and pop culture, were ever ugly? How can skin rich in melanin, a natural protectant from the sun's aging power, ever be considered anything but elite? A society fueled by white supremacy, combined with jealousy and fear, had tricked the world, and even me, into thinking I was not beautiful.

Today, it is ever so obvious that Black women are beautiful. Just simply getting online reminds anyone of the ways in which we stand as a blueprint for beauty, expression, and quite literally, culture. But validation from a society that now mimics Black womanhood hasn't always been as readily accessible. And for that reason, many of us—Black women—are still grappling with our past traumas and unlearning the hate we were fed. To those Black women, and to my younger self, I do not have a recommendation other than to enjoy the journey of falling in love with yourself. It is the most beautiful experience of all.

A LOVE LETTER TO MY BLACKNESS, WHICH I FINALLY UNDERSTAND

BY JAYNE ALLEN

was called "Black," but for the longest time, especially as a child, I had no idea what you were. I knew to check for you in paper boxes. While you awaited my embrace, I imagined you with the "if you knew what I know" kind of smile perfected by grandmothers who sewed quilts and made butter pound cakes and steaming pots of collard greens all on the same day.

From my time of pigtails to press-and-curls, you waited patiently for me to notice you, to perceive your value. Like me, the late bloomer whose beauty was on delay, eager for recognition.

I hoped and prayed for long, straight hair and had a relationship with the sun that ignored the power of my melanin. I was careful with my diction, immaculate with grammar, and was sure I could achieve my way out of any predicament. *Good grades have no color*, I was told.

I thought—because that's what everyone told me to think—you and I were the last chosen, the least desired, the ones with the most to prove.

I was an awkward teenager unsure of where I fit in. You made your own place in the world. Still, we became friends. I could bet on you to have all the best music, so generously shared—the soul, the funk, the highest notes, the smoothest crooning, the window-shaking bass, the Prince, the kings, and all the queens. You lived life in the brightest colors.

We started to have fun together. You were an entry into the greatest times of my life. Parties where everyone danced on the even beats. Food that lit up my mouth in every dimension. Jokes that snapped so hard I had to double over to get all the laugh out.

But I never loved you deeply. At least, not until I found myself in Washington, DC, one day with time on my hands. There, I visited the Smithsonian Museum of African American History. On the bottom floor, I encountered the Middle Passage. I traveled up through time, through enslavement, then abolition, then Reconstruction. I met the Jim Crow refugees, the civil rights survivors (plus those who were not), the eminent domain withstanders (and those who could not) until finally, after hours of walking through every reason why there should be no me, all I could see was you.

You are the me that made it through. Distilled excellence, my Blackness—you are not a shadow but the light instead that shines through darkness, illuminating my steps. You are the part of me that will always find a way forward.

My love for you is an ever-expanding appreciation. I dance you, eat you, speak you, write you, wear you, bathe you in the sun, lavish you in shea butter, and laugh in the way that you laugh until my belly hurts and the tears fall. And I cry for you. I march for you, still. I pray for you, for your freedom, and for mine.

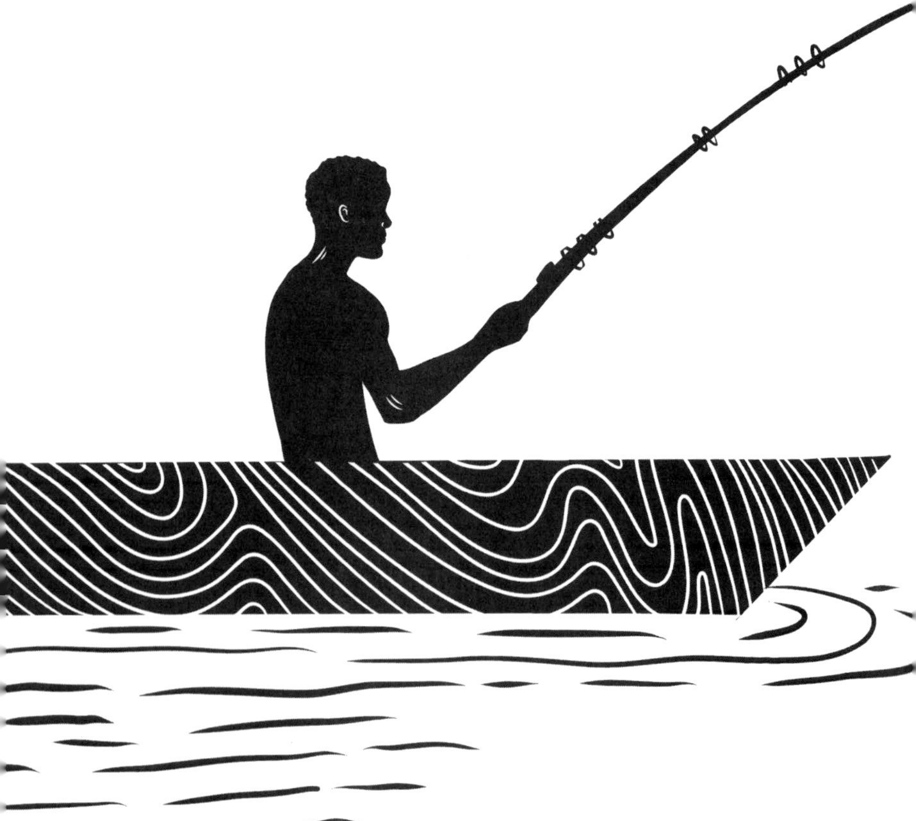

FISHING

BY KWAME DAWES

‖ CHASM

The day's heat still clings despite the growing gloom.
It is twilight. The lake stretches dumbly here in the gut
   of the state. We push off—the ritual is calming.
      Our orange life jackets, the ballasting of the child
        in blankets to cradle her when the undulating
          water rocks her softly; and you sitting at the helm
           peering out, your back to me. I have tried to read
           its stoic guardedness, but the language is glutted
           by resentments. On the drive down we talked
         of bills, the schedule ahead, words arriving
        without prompting as if trying to empty
      ourselves of the ordinary, the chafe, before
     the wide silence of the water. Now, on the lake,
you hum psalms. I have learned the science of baiting
in the dark. My line hisses, then grows silent.
I wait for the tug, the feel of life beneath us.

133

You are a shadow across the divide. A child
sleeps between us like a bridge. It is easier
to smell you: the fresh sweat, the faint cologne—
than to feel you. To catch bass, you must
pray softly, remain still, allow the dark
to lull you before the pull. Tonight, nothing
bites. I am rehearsing my tears and speeches
now—the fear that beneath this placid
familiar surface is a void so complete,
so irrevocably grand in its silences, it could
drown us. I doze off from the heat
and the metronome of the lapping water—
then sleeping, I awake to find you gone; the girl
on a pillow floating among the reeds and rushes,
the moon growing over me. It is fleeting.
I regret the relief I feel. I wake again when you say,
"Let's go home. It's late."

 GETTING THERE

After John Sargent's *Paul Helleu Sketching with His Wife*

He rows alone, planting slicked worn wood
softly into the current. He is mesmerized
by the sound of parting, the whisper

of moving water against the weathered flanks
of the boat. She stares into the sky,
holding close to her chest the damp
paddle—it soaks into the fabric,
then into her skin; her pout is gone—
she is cold already; fights no longer
sustain her, stir her. He grunts.
"We are fighting the order of things;
you keep losing the rhythm. We will
go in circles if you don't let me do it."
How can she say to this logic,
"I dreamt we were doing it together.
I saw us moving with something
delicious, the pull and tug of lovers—
I imagined us cutting the surface like this
or at least trying and laughing about it"?
So, he does, and at last the romance:
a lazy summer dusk, the moon growing
over the swamp's edge, the water
near tepid, a sullen amiable sluggishness,
the straw hats, the red ribbons,
the sports jacket, the wide skirt,
the satchel of paints and brushes,
the accoutrements of a picnic,
the orderliness of a boat drifting
across a placid lake, the pewter

and sepia rocks to the side. She says,
"Yes, you do it. I will watch."
He will ask her if she is happy,
if she enjoyed the water, the view;
if she found his landscape, the humid
watercolor of a stunted dogwood
lovely and to her liking. She hears,
"Did you come?" and she answers
as always with faith, "It was lovely;
you were lovely"—for that is enough.
She is holding the paddle to her breasts,
the hard handle pressing her nipple—
it will leave a mark on her skin.

 CATCH

There is in that sudden elation of a catch,
a belief in miracles, a wide open light
as wide as hope. For an instant, the dark,
the placid dense quiet, the gap between
lovers islanded on a boat drifting
over a lake, forty miles away from light,
from the miniature city where his mother
waits with bowls of seasoned flour,
diced onions, peppers, and garlic,

a cleared counter and a deep pot
of still oil waiting on the stove. She watches
reruns of soaps, waiting for him to come
with the fresh catch—a faith in his return
always firm—a kind of conjuring
that bemuses all other distractions.
This is what you think about here
on the lake—a mockery of this silence
between lovers, before the exquisite
chaos of a bite, then the grunt and cheers
of hauling it in. The gift arrives with
laughter and tears; who could imagine
such elation in this gleaming tangible
thing? He hands it to you and you
can be forgiven for seeing him as a man,
strong provider, hunter, and progenitor;
forgiven for the softening of pride
you feel—the dampness in your eyes.
In that instance you imagine the breaking
of ties, the un-cleaving from a mother's
elastic umbilicus reaching across the miles.
You are in love again, in this interim,
before you say, "Let me put it back."
And he says, "We are keeping this."
And you say, "We have eaten already."
And he says, "For mother. She is waiting."

IV NOCTURNAL

There in the quiet of midnight, the body cleansed
of the detritus of gutted fish, only the iron smell
of blood still lingering in the nose—the house
is still rocking like a boat; he is snoring—everything
ticks with creaturely disquiet. You think
of the anatomy of orgasms—how they change each
time; how narrow they have become—the closed
walls of pleasure. These days it is something fierce
like resentful pain—a moment with no elasticity.
The after effect is mute, a dull high; the kind
junkies must feel long after the first giddy years of surprise.
You are able now to contemplate afterwards,
the menu for tomorrow, the errands, chores,
the cat litter you must buy, the eggs, the milk,
the poem you must write. Those long
transportations that took you into the misty,
stomach-unfurling, body-thorough fatigue
are gone—those days when all you could think
was when the nervous pulsing would stop,
when the distended bloat and sweet pain
would subside, when your breath would
return to something ordinary, when the skin
would not jump at the breath of a breeze

or the suggestion of touch—all gone.
Now the body aches with the labor.
Now you shout harshly, almost a bark.
Now you don't care who hears; you say,
maybe at least they will envy me, which
is better than not. Now you grind out
your desire like a short flame: fast, then done.
Dreams, though, multiply these days;
they come even while you are awake;
they come with the rush of clouds.
You collect art, pictures of women—
hundreds of them. You stare long enough
at their complex of colors, then enter worlds
so far from your ordinary days. You float
through these distractions with a gladness;
something like the way you swim,
head underwater, eyes closed tight, arms
moving furiously, the air pressed against
your chest. The sound is deep green,
and you push forward hoping for the assurance
of the bank. But as you move forward,
you are suspended in this postcard painting of a fish
cutting through tendrils and reeds, light
whipping past, the world, pleasant as that old,
glorious orgasm that used to unfold and unfold
for hours and hours and hours.

 **MARIANA**

After John Everett Millais's *Mariana*

There is a fresh Christian sincerity in hooking bass,
then unhooking the dumb mouths, feeling the muscle
of desperation in your hand. Then after pictures,
you plant them in the lake, holding on long enough
to feel the sensuality of water, warm in this June
season—the living pulsation before letting go—
bass falling into ritual, another lesson of grace
lost on it. Your hands make things—embroidery
of such gothic elaboration, a prayer cloth
stretched over your prayer table strewn with
leaves that have spilled through the stained-glass
window that overlooks your garden.
At dusk, after the shower, after the ordering
of the household, you stand, arms akimbo
before the window, looking out as if you
expect someone to be looking back, and you avert
your gaze casually, waiting for the last light
to flame your skin into that mellow brownness,
a color so full of beauty that it startled you
once as you walked past a store window.
You wear your navy-blue gown, the one

that clings close to your torso. The waist
where your hands rest is smaller, and you
thrust your breast forward, the white frills
framing the soft gutter of your bosom—
you give this to the window, to the garden,
to the light. You are fishing for a compliment;
your reflection against the speckled window
seduces. But it is growing dark now.
A grey bass is plunging deeply into the hollow
of the lake. There is hunger in your body's quiet
desire that offers no language. You smell
the living death of fish in your fingers.
The prayer cloth is unfinished; you work,
the crochet needles moving in quick blurs
like the breaking of the lake before
the boat's bow. At dawn, you will
cover your head, whisper a prayer while soft
light catches you in dark garments
like a girl returning from the clandestine party,
ready to repent of all her terrible sins.

 **ADDICTION**

I have grown to love the rituals of fishing. Addiction
is too dramatic an analogy, but my routine has changed

and I am drawn to the open lake in this dense
heat of summer like I am drawn to those vices
that always left me hungry, tender, and wondering
what the next time will be like. I sit in the kitchen
and the impulse crawls up my legs like a voice
would whisper its way into my damp places.
I allow air in, a reflex to cool the slow burn.
It never stops until I stand, walk to the window,
stare into the sky, looking east to Sumter, as if
I can see across the swamp, the untidy pine
forest, the trailer parks, then the long wood-thick
road that falls open at the muddy landing.
I calculate the clouds' weight, testing their messy
smudges of pewter, charcoal, indigo, and gray
to see how long I can stay dry there on the open
water, my lure settled low, my mind caught
in the suspended place between air and the dark
mystery of the lake's belly. The fear is still
there; I still tremble at the nudge of drifting
vegetation against the boat's skin, tremble
as if it is my body being invaded. But I can
speak to the mute watery shadows beneath
the surface; and there on the water, my pulse
slows to a drugged slumber—all things
move with the sluggish labor of a hawk
rising into the sky, above the pine needles.

I drive the rain-slick road, leaving it all behind.
The nearer I come to the water, the more
I understand myth—how a girl could talk to fish,
kiss fish, embrace the slimy fulsomeness
of a speckled bass—how me, a squeamish girl,
can enter this soft muggy world of earth smells,
blood, and the ammonia scent of dead fish;
how she can, in this place, find comfort
and the sweet release of addiction.

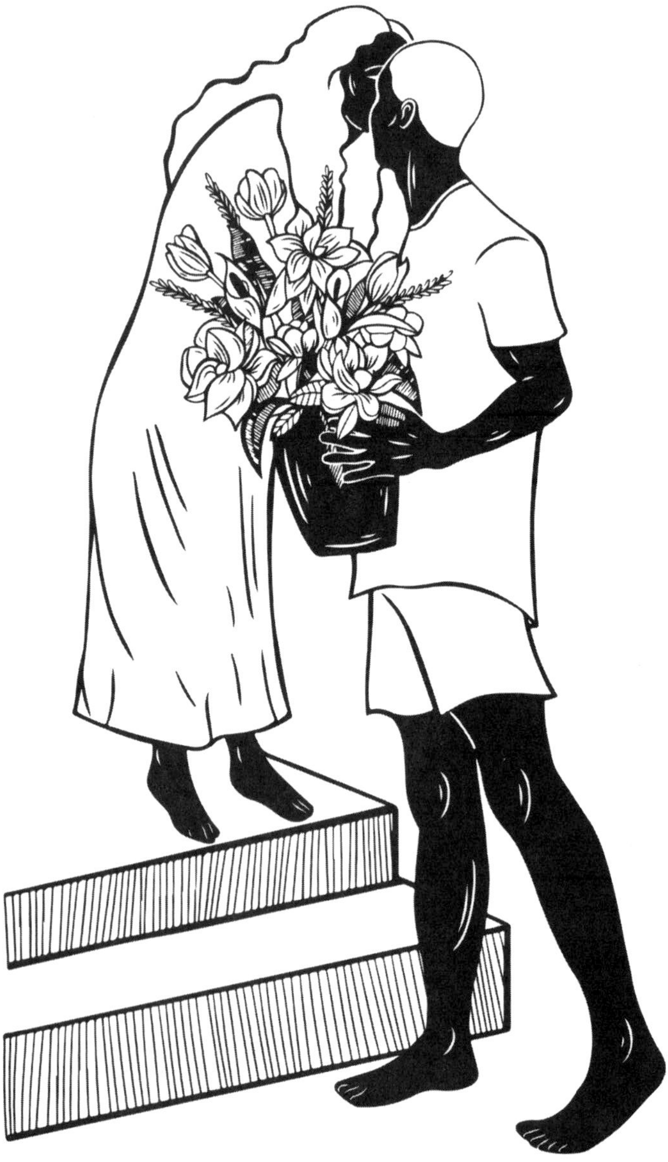

IRONWOMAN

BY COLE BROWN

We call you *Mama*, though *Chef* and *Doctor* and *Dad* would all suit. *Captain* too, the way you steered us through the storms of adolescence, divorce, losses of lives and innocence.

The world thinks you're strong—ironclad. Which you are—of will and spirit and resolve—but of body, you're frail. The world may not know that, but I do. I see you wince and hear your groans. You insist there was a time before your delicacy when you could run and jump and swim like the others. I believe you, then strain to imagine, but I have only ever known you as you are now. And for that reason, I have always suspected that I won't have you for long. When we part for long stretches, I have a hunch that it will be for the last time.

I know what I'd say though, should the worst come to pass. I'd ask the congregation to sit up in their seats, real straight and still. I'd tell 'em all to remember that we in the house of the Lord, so they better be honest because they wouldn't be lying to me, they'd be lying to God hisself, and He'd know the difference, and today is a real good day for smiting.

Then I'd say, *If she warmed your insides, please stand.*

145

And they all would. *Of course* they would. Even the jerk next door and the drunk bitch in Paris that called us *nègres* and the boss that started Trump-trippin' and the triflin' cousins, siblings, and friends, and your ex-husband with mixed memories. The world that thought you strong.

I'd feel that warmth. Your last flicker.

And then I'd say, *If she made the grass grow, please stand.*

And I'd be the only one standing again—me and the little girl that leaned on you like I did. Just us two.

Then the terror.

What now?

Fear of loss—that's my love for you.

POPS AND DAD

BY VJ JENKINS

We had that kind of friendship that deserves a story—Black, boyish, infinite, unruly, and unrestricted. In our minds we were the homies in *ATL*, *Boyz n the Hood*, *The Wood*, *The Best Man*—we had that *Bud, Not Buddy* spit-bond. And our story goes like all of those, with the pain and loss that complement the naivety of young fools thinking they can forever be unencumbered by life paths diverging.

I would go back to then if I could. Innocent. Laughing all night as we compared ass-whooping stories. You remember the flag football games and bonfires or the time you fell out of the tree playing flashlight tag? God, we laughed! And the early Sunday texts to make sure you were coming to church, because what was church if we couldn't laugh together at folks catching the Holy Ghost. We laughed so many big laughs. The trampoline, the busted nose, the hole in the basement door, the Coke stain on the floor, Ma's constant threat to jack you up, sneaking out of windows to find trouble together. My house and our childhood stories—I know you are laughing to yourself as each one of those memories flood back.

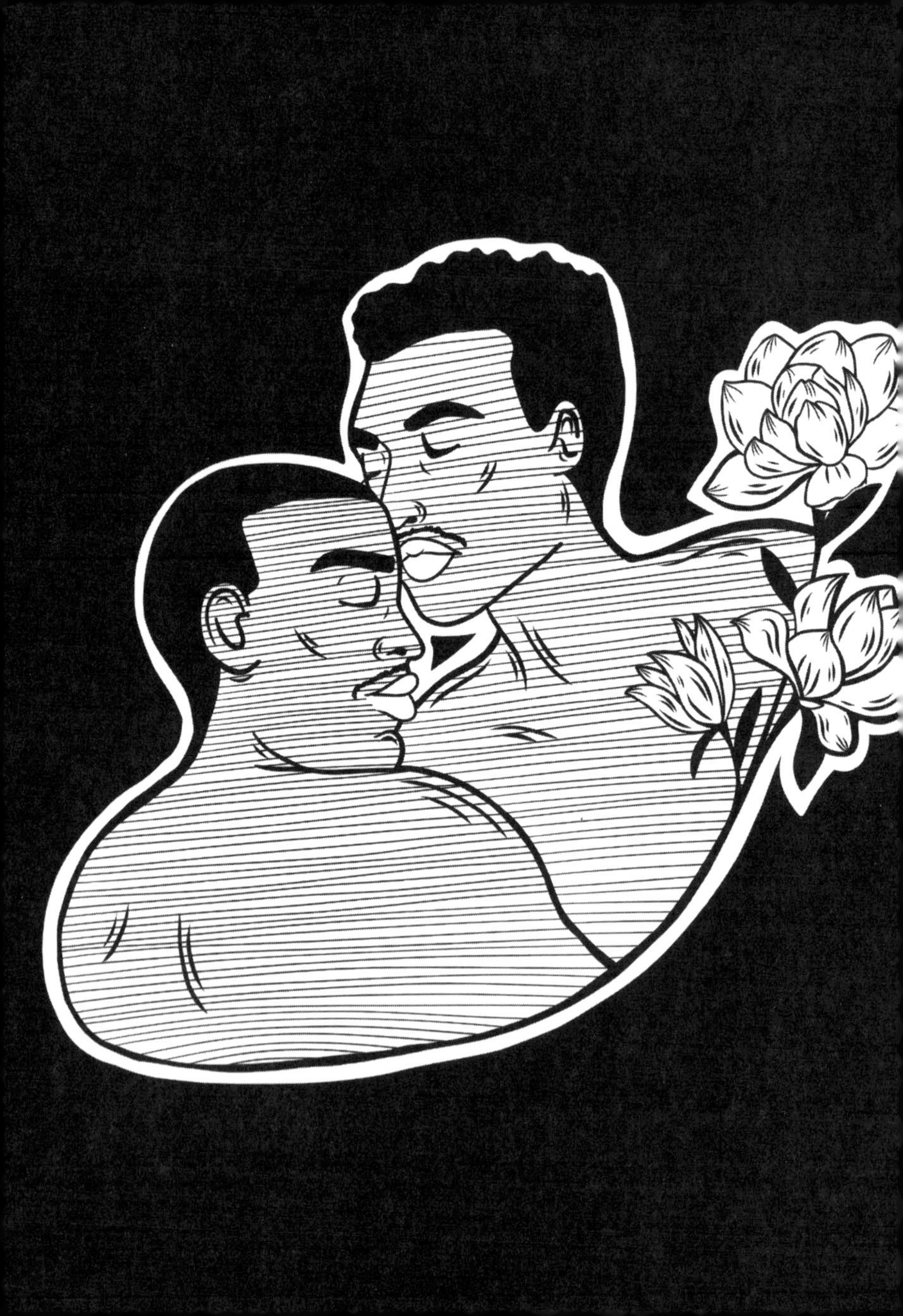

Then, Paris interrupted us for a while. You left, and I couldn't understand that sting or ache that accompanied the forced separation. It made me feel uneasy and unclean. Whatever I was feeling didn't make sense in relation to boys at the time. So I fought to tuck it away with hate and rage and confusion building up inside. Why did I need you? How could I miss you like that? *God, no, that's not me!*

I counted down the days until my visit with angst and urge. I vividly remember the first time we walked the streets of Paris smoking by the river. I was enthralled by the city, the high . . . and you. And that night, something happened that wasn't supposed to happen between boys, especially Black boys. Now, we had a secret hidden from the world, together.

And maybe that's what makes this love letter foolish. This story has been written. But I didn't know it wouldn't work. It wasn't on the TV then, and I hadn't read Baldwin or Broome or Moore. I thought we were supposed to hide it, and hate it. But that thing that happened in Paris happened again. And then again, many more times as we continued to navigate high school. So I started to imagine our one day. You were going to be Pops, and I was going to be Dad. And it was going to be beautiful—eventually.

But we continued to practice our performance art of talking to women. We hid love well under the sheets—door shut and lights off. That's the cruelty of loving you. It's always been hidden. Even now, I can't use your name.

It hurt. Often. That time I caressed your hand as we walked the aisle of the grocery store, hoping you'd return a playful smile but was scolded with a brisk, "What the fuck!"

Every time I tried to emerge into myself, I got thrust backward. Because my understanding of me was tied to you. It was we, us, our, completely entangled in my mind. All I wanted was to reach out to you and say, *I am here. Take my hand.* I wanted to embrace our young Black love.

But, just as suddenly as it all started, those thoughts of a happily ever after came to an end. I, a college Sophomore, still hoped—you, a newly minted Navy man, moved on. And you called with that news that crushed the entirety of me. She was pregnant. You were getting married. And he arrived in the world, a beautiful child. I was an "uncle" now to the boy that came into this world and crushed mine, and I had to find love for him, because he was your baby boy.

But even still, as we near thirty, promising visits that never happen, I want you. I want to grow old with you, laughing about the time we've wasted apart like in our favorite movie, *Life.* I want us to rewrite Giovanni's curse. So if you ever reach out your hand in love, I'll grab it. Forever ever. And I'll be Dad. And you'll be Pops. And our kids will see love between us, and for us. Because the world is changing. Our love letter doesn't have to end with "only if we lived in a different time." But I don't think you can love the part of me that loves you. The part that still hopes. The part that is willing to say, *I am gay.*

It's no longer a cancer I want to cut out. It no longer seems antithetical to my Black masculinity. It is beautiful to be Black, to be man, and to be gay. I don't know if this is a love letter to you or to me. But ours was a love story that ended with me smiling, because I love the part of me that you ignited.

PS: Every time you call, I am shocked by how debilitatingly overwhelmed I become with a sense of home, past, longing, and happiness. After all this time, your voice is enough. I am forever sorry if publishing this letter is the end of those calls.

V

TRANSFORMATION

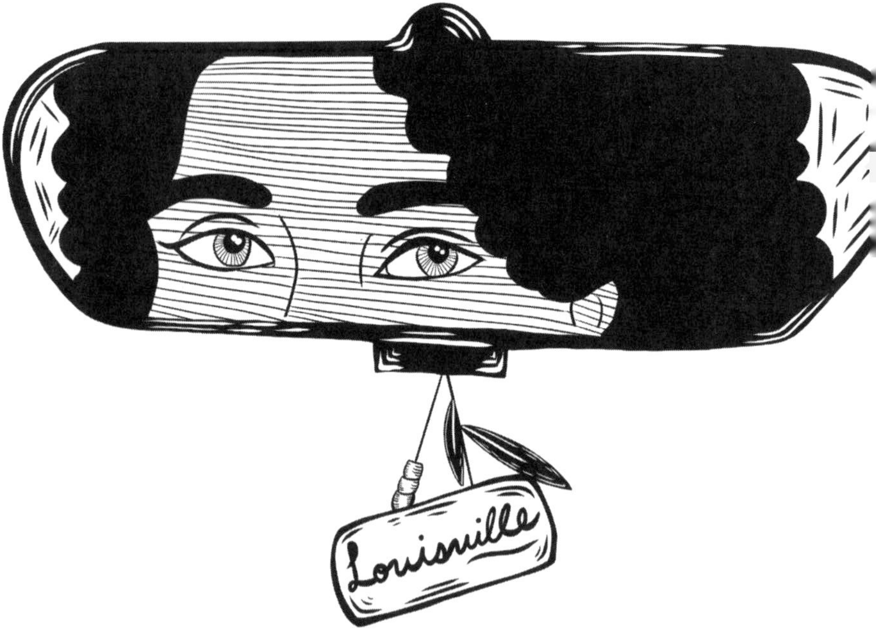
Louisville

HOME: A RECKONING

BY TRACEY MICHAE'L LEWIS-GIGGETTS

DEAR LOUISVILLE,

Your gravel-gray streets call out to me at times. Some days, the sound is garbled, reflecting the confusion I feel when I think of you. Other days, your voice is glorious. A reminder of our early days when this little brown girl with braids and beads that snapped and cracked when I turned my head, with tiny pieces of aluminum foil holding those same beads in place, would scream with excitement as she watched the Belle of Louisville ease on down the river or the Pegasus Parade bands march on by. I remember my heart swelling at the sight of the twinkling lights downtown at the Galleria. Or how that same twinkle showed up in my eyes as I held sparklers, my absolute favorite, at my family's Derby cookout. This much I know for sure: The woman I am is a result of the girl I was. The girl you raised.

. . .

I remember being four. Not the normal four. Not the Barbie-playing, ABC-singing, cartwheel-flipping kind of four. I was . . . as my granny used to say . . . four going on thirty-four. She said this because quietly it was her fault. She was my sitter for the first few years of my life, and most of our days in Bent Creek Apartments were spent watching *The Young and the Restless* and *Star Trek*, talking to her girlfriends about what so-and-so did the previous weekend, and inhaling the scent of Virginia Slims and brown liquor.

Oh, and talking about white folks.

"Can't trust 'em," Ms. Violet would say. A pretty woman with smooth almond skin, I don't think I ever remember her not wearing a full face of makeup.

"I ain't attracted to 'em either," Granny would chime in. "Except maybe that Bond guy."

"Ooooh, child, yes! Sean Connery. I could definitely . . ."

"Shhh! Hush now! The baby."

Painted eyes would fall on me as I pretended to play with the random high heel shoe, the furry fringes on the couch pillows, or the plastic carpet running in the long hallway.

"Oh and the one from *The Way We Were*."

"Robert Redford!"

"Yessss, child!"

Cackles of laughter, high fives, secret words, and knowing glances would follow.

This is Louisville to me. This is my memory of you. The way you take shape in my brain. How you fill my heart.

. . .

I know when people think of Kentucky, their minds turn to sleek and brown horses or bluegrass. Maybe even mint juleps and big hats. All the things you sell them. But that is not my experience of you, old friend. In my corner of you, it was fish fries, barbecue ribs, and pinochle. Tonk and spades games. It was fountains at the Belvedere after church on Sundays. It was slow rides through Shawnee Park. It was also heartache and rejection. It was sexual abuse and religious dogma. It was racism and subtle messages of inferiority.

But, of course, when I was five years old, you couldn't have told me that you weren't the biggest, most majestic city on the planet. When a place is all you've known, it's all you can imagine. Sure, I would later learn that cities like New York and Chicago and London existed, but even then, the comparison felt, still feels, inadequate because I think what I understood even as a kindergartner is that skyscrapers and subways don't indicate how big a place is in one's heart. And "The Ville" is BIG big in mine—in the best and worst ways.

Even when I didn't know it, couldn't see it, was sheltered from it, you were always the place where a Breonna Taylor could find herself counting bullets instead of sheep. The place where my own elder cousin, Vickie Lee Jones, would never finish grocery shopping because a white man would decide that she should die because she was Black. You were always that place too. Also.

You are the site of so much pain.

You are the site of so much joy.

And reconciling those two realities feels like the undertaking of a lifetime. A journey I choose to take with the support of a therapist or three.

．　．　．

We're off to see the Wizard . . .

When I first breached your borders, running away with my oyster knife in hand, I was in search of a world that would love me better. I felt very much like Dorothy in my own twisted, late-twentieth-century version of *The Wizard of Oz*. It was 1997 and I never had any intentions of returning. Not in any real way. Just for the occasional in-and-out visits with family and friends. I was determined that you would never have my heart again. But then I grew up. I realized that the Wizard I was looking for to make me okay was not real. And if there ever was a Wizard, he was pointing me home. It was time for reckoning and recompense and repentance. It was time to feel again.

The only way we ever really know we've been numb, emotionally, is when we actually start feeling again. When the tingles come. It's one of those "be careful what you ask for" moments. Now, when I come home to you, I feel everything. Intense emotions overtake me as I remember who you were, who you are. When I consider who I was, who I am. When I think about who we are both becoming.

Our relationship is by definition complicated. I left you as one does a place that can no longer serve them. No longer hold their tears. But the love never dies, does it? In between the terrors, I now see your beauty. The way you fortified me for this work I do. These words I write. The way you taught me who I can be and also who I never wanted to be. How you ensured that I never lost hope.

I have found my gratitude. It was buried beneath my rage and grief.

Every time I return now, I watch you grow. There are new names for old roads. More diverse groups of people have settled into your streets and avenues. Every journey back forces me to remember and run. To run back and tell six- and eleven- and fifteen-year-old Tracey that no matter what it looks like, we are safe. We figure it out eventually. We will one day stop running. I'm reminded that while I may have left Louisville, Louisville has never left me.

Sometimes when I return to you, I find myself opening one of my mother's million photo albums. The kind with intricate designs on the cover and the sticky paper inside that holds the actual prints in place. There's one pic of me I always gravitate toward. My hair is out and wild and I'm sitting on a Sit 'n Spin, mid-turn, and my smile is wide and free. I stare at that little girl. She is me. At three. The corners of the yellowed photo reach out to me; folding toward my heart space in a symbol of how long ago it had been since I'd known her. Me.

That photo represents part of how I see you, my City. As a place that lives inside of me, but I have to dig deep to reach.

You know how it feels when you meet someone for the first time and your stomach becomes all gooey with anticipation and you wonder if this will be the one, if this will be the time you will be loved the way you deserve and, ultimately, maybe, you are disappointed, or maybe you just realize that some people and, yes, even some places, have limited capacities. They can only hold so much of who you have become, and so you forgive them. Over and over again. I extend grace to you, Louisville, always and always. I will keep coming back with my hope and love tucked close. After nearly a half century of living, I have made my peace.

> *From Shawnee Park to Hurstbourne Lane*
> *(I mean, Parkway), I love you.*
> *Tracey*

DEAR SELF:
A LETTER OF WITNESSING

BY ALEXANDRA ELLE

DEAR SELF,

I see you in new ways now. I love you for who you are and who you aren't. Each step you've walked has gotten you here, and I can finally say that I honor you: your strength, softness, and healing. I see and respect it all. Each facet of you shines. Your light is undeniable. The road to becoming has not been easy, and it won't get easier as you grow, but what's so beautiful about this walk is trusting the season. Every shedding and blooming teaches us something about being able to let go in order to heal, change, and grow.

I see your truth.
I see your vulnerability.
I see your pain.
I see your uncertainty.
I see your willingness to try.

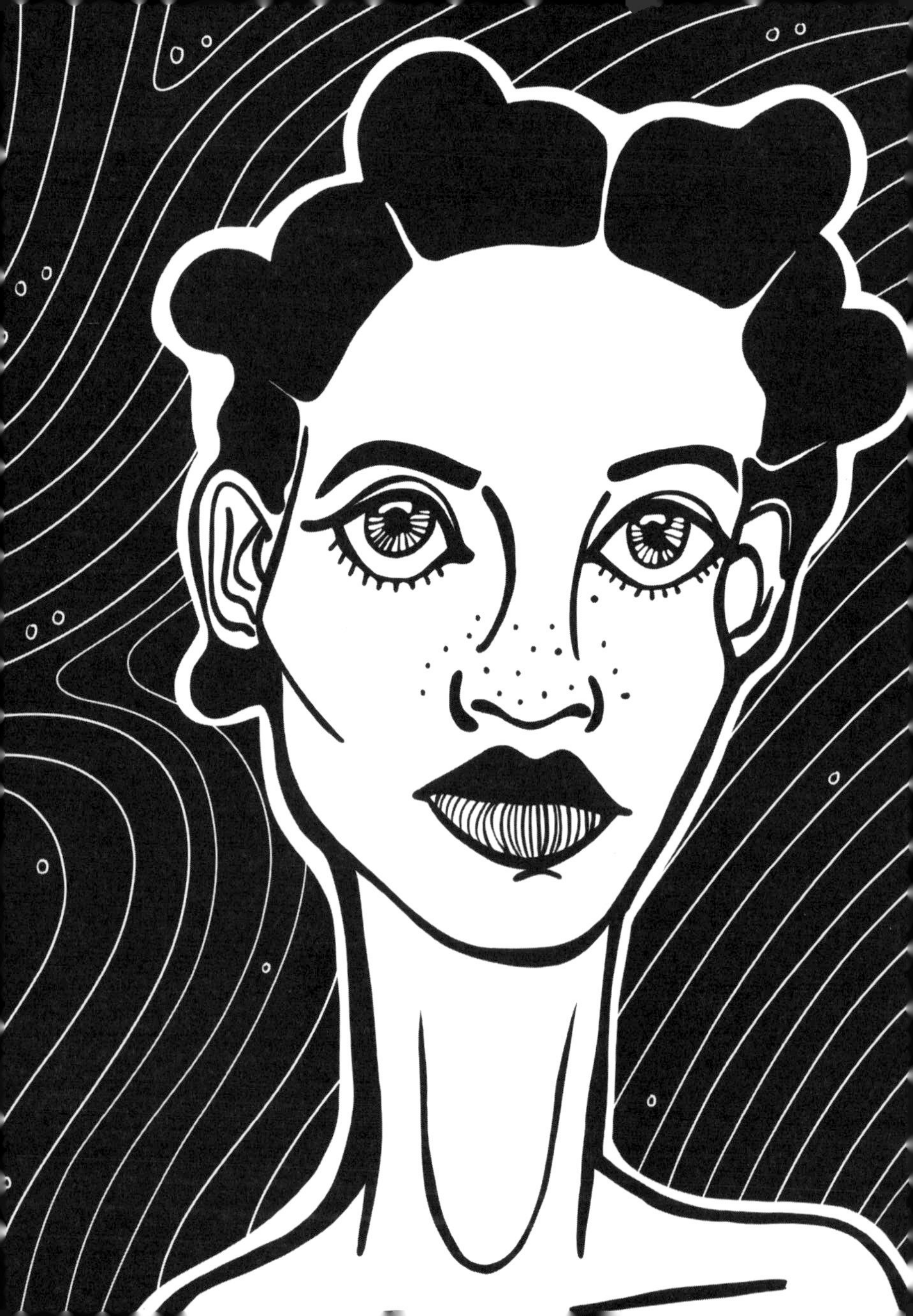

I see your openness to healing.
I see your commitment to growth.
I see your dedication to being who you didn't have.

There is so much beauty to witness on this journey. Seeing you so clearly be yourself is something I've been waiting for.

We are reveling in this glory together.

You are clear about what you no longer want.
You are clear about what needs to be released.
You are making room for what is in alignment with your growth.

That is sacred work.
That is self-nurturing embodied, and I am proud of you.

I see you in alignment with your highest good.
I see you moving intentionally in the direction of your life's purpose.

You are beautiful to witness. My eyes are open.

I see you in new and illuminating ways now. I love you for who you are and who you will be.

In gratitude and compassion,

Self

LOVE AND IMAGINATION

BY DEBORAH WILLIS

Deborah Willis's son is acclaimed conceptual artist Hank Willis Thomas.

DEAR HANK,

I received a letter inviting us to speak at the TEDWomen conference in New Orleans on November 1, 2017. They asked if you would be able to join me in a conversation at the Orpheum Theater in the French Quarter. Let's say *yes*. The theme is on *Bridges*, e.g., we build them, we traverse them, and sometimes we even burn them, for better or worse. For me, a TED Talk is a humbling experience, and to share our stories and experiences with a public we are unfamiliar with is unthinkable. Let's do it as I love our collaborations and especially your new project "LoveOverRules." Pat Mitchell's invitation is a heartwarming one as a mother/son project. Let's focus our project on love.

These are *desperate* moments in our lives and your project "LoveOverRules" is a significant intervention. That word *desperate* is an *adjective*. A description, and yet it can feel like a noun.

What *word* does an artist have to offer, or *tools* do they hold in their hand, eyes, and tongue to go to battle against such a word?

I submit with two words—LOVE and IMAGINATION.

As long as artists have an imagination, they are free to reshape and reconsider where we want and need to be, and take us there. With that, they show us our value; show us that our lives matter.

It is an honor for me to be able to collaborate with you. Your professor and my friend, Professor Robin D. G Kelley, wrote an article that I often ask my students to read. I remember these three words: Love-Study-Struggle. These words are central to me as well. We must love the work that we are doing in pursuit of beauty and justice, and to do so we must embrace the struggle, and continue to study and participate in making our lives matter.

As you have witnessed, my career has consistently been art-centered. I am committed to making art, researching, sharing, and writing. *What can we learn from artists? Are the Arts essential?* are questions that motivate me, my work, and much of my thinking. Whether I'm organizing an exhibition, a thematic conference, writing a book, or even preparing a new syllabus each semester, these questions guide and encourage me. I have always viewed artists as teachers and leaders—because we are curious, we have a desire to make changes and seek new possibilities. Amiri Baraka wrote that possibilities move us. I strongly agree.

As an artist, mom, and curator, I have sought an active role in creating exchanges of perspectives about art and culture, and how art engages with questions we face as a society today. My experience as an academic has reaffirmed my belief that the arts have a crucial role to play in imagining new futures, especially in turbulent times such as these. Whether they do so as creative practices that directly engage with social and environmental issues or through the quiet, focused work in the studio, dark-room, or lab, the arts are essential in helping us think in subtle and bold ways about what it is and can mean to be human.

In 1955, your grandmother, my mom, decided that she wanted to be a beautician and enrolled in the Apex Beauty School on South Broad Street in South Philadelphia. I studied art and pho-tography a block away from there some twenty years later. Her interest in working in the beauty industry was supported by all the women in our family and your granddad. In that shop, mom opened her doors to dreamers, churchwomen, singers, dancers, domestic workers, bankers and clubwomen, quilters, musicians, artists, and their daughters. It was a place full of love, visual stimulations from magazines, books, and posters, where women waited and caught up on the local and national news, and the gossip—a place where women had a chance to be heard. This introduced me to a world of women's stories, which would assert itself as a prominent feature of my creative work. All these women were my surrogate babysitters, teachers, role models.

I remember sitting in that shop after mom's graduation and reading the magazines and listening to the stories. I recall picking up one book and noting the title: *Men of Mark*—I was intrigued by that title, and I quietly thought about what it means to leave a mark!

I remember mom reciting a poem by Langston Hughes: "Life for me ain't been no crystal stair." Those words planted themselves in my eyes from early on, in that space dedicated to preserving, continuing, and extending the beauty of these women who sat in its chairs, defeating anything outside its doors that said anything different. And where I began to imagine my own place in that preservation of beauty and how I would continue that, how would I leave my mark. How could I become a Woman of Mark?

It's important to say to you in this letter how I developed my art practice over time, as I see you adding your voice.

I knew early on that I wanted to tell visual stories and become a photographer. I read the pictures and began to imagine the text. I believed that experience helped to shape my vision today.

As you probably remember, I grew up in a house filled with hope—filled with stories, music and art, and other forms of creativity found in the kitchen, in the living room, and at the sewing machine. I have always been sensitive to artistic expressions and my passion has always been focused on photography and storytelling.

I thought when I entered the Philadelphia College of Art in the 1970s that I needed to pursue a dual career—as a practicing artist and scholar in the arts, focusing on the works and careers of Black photographers. That was because of the lack of information and exhibitions on Black artists during that time. When I attended PCA, there were only two Black women in the photography program. I was confronted with a professor who informed me that I was "taking up a good man's space." I credit PCA with helping me to create a different community of artists because I had to battle to keep my voice heard. And eventually I MADE SPACE for a Good Man—you.

I ran into your friend Nekisha Durrett when I was in DC recently. She had been on my mind as I've witnessed her develop her voice and vision from afar. I asked her, "Nekisha, what did you think of me when you were a child hanging out at our house?" Her response:

> I remember that I thought I knew no one else like you. I remember you were surrounded by books and beautiful, humble objects that held so much meaning. Every time I touched something, it was like I pressed the Hank activation button and he would spring up like a docent, "You know that is so-and-so's bench?? That's Josephine Baker's table."
>
> I remember you writing and going places.
> I remember you loving your work!
> I had never really known a grown-up who loved their work.
> In a word, I thought you were FREE. I love you and thank you.

I laughed out loud when I read these words and cried.

My message as an artist has always been the same—in search of beauty. I communicate the message of beauty by organizing conferences and exhibitions as well as publishing books. In my view, we are all responsible for our future, which we must bring through our art.

Your contribution toward making a difference in the practice of art is crucial, we need your vision and voice to continue to build on the foundation we know from our history of creating, writing, reading, and curating in the arts. Continue to uncover new interpretations in old text. You and your generation are our future, our change agents. Imagine the possibility. Just imagine fifty years ago we would have never thought of hip-hop as a canon. Because of its magic there are numerous exhibitions celebrating the fiftieth anniversary. Baltimore Museum of Art, *The Culture: Hip Hop and Contemporary Art in the 21st Century*, and in New York, *Hip-Hop: Conscious, Unconscious* and *Fresh, Fly, and Fabulous: 50 Years of Hip Hop Style*.

You have a warehouse of possibilities. Continue to make Magic a reality with your "LoveOverRules" installations.

Love you,
Mom

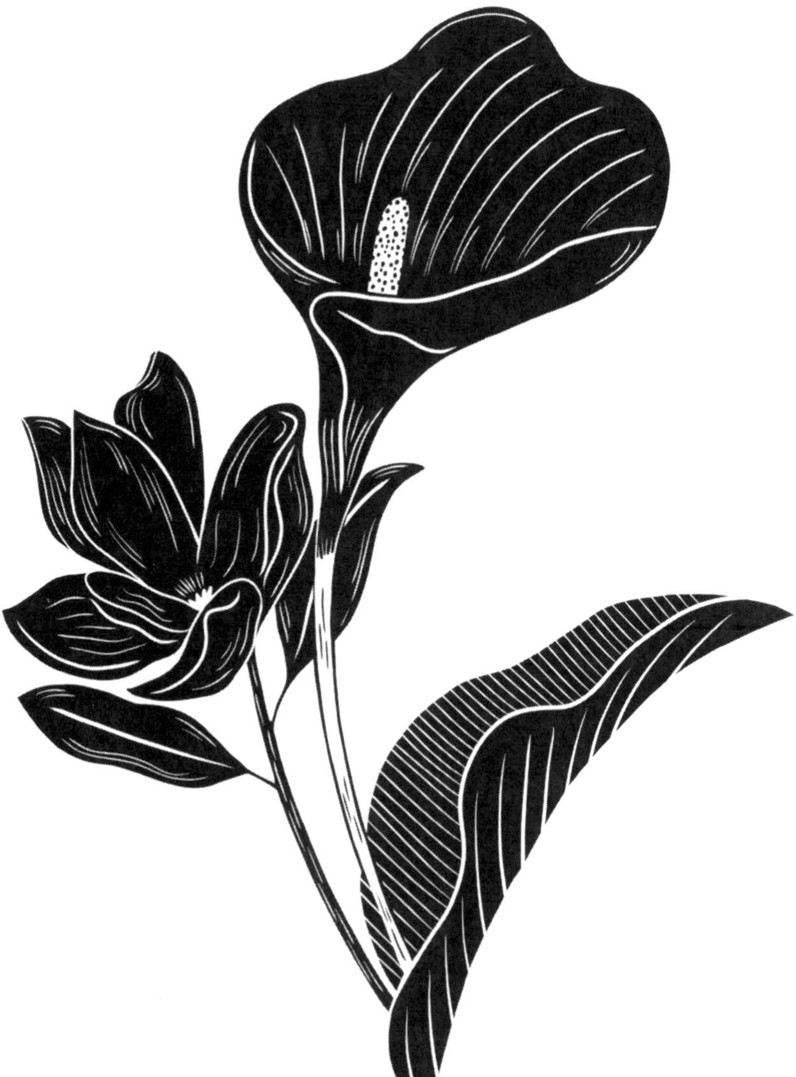

DEAR ELEVEN-YEAR-OLD MICHAEL JACKSON

BY BRONTEZ PURNELL

First of all, I wanna say, I LOVE YOU I LOVE YOU I LOVE YOU I LOVE YOU. You are my future dad, I am your future son, you are my future child, I am your future dad. This helix of space-time cannot contain the gifts and glory of its inhabitants— and why should it try? I have believed in you since before I could talk or articulate how it made me feel when I was but five and had a documentary tape of your 1969 appearance on *The Ed Sullivan Show* and you are but eleven years old, wearing that big-ass purple hat and doing a rendition of "Who's Lovin' You" with the conviction of someone three times your age. I still love you, actually, and I don't care who knows that.

No for real, what can I say that wouldn't fall short of the glory? I mean, I think we should start with the basics: you are eleven and have no way of knowing that within the first one hundred years of broadcast media, YOU ALONE will be the most televised Black man in this very contained window of history. Don't forget that. More so, in a country where a few short years ago, you, little eleven-year-old Black boy, couldn't even get a soda at the bar or a dinner or a drink from the "wrong" water fountain—oh shit, fuck, JESUS—even sit at the front of the bus. Hell, you were just barely able to come through the front door of the first venues you played on stage in. I know that you are only eleven—just shy of twelve—but even now, when you've barely reached puberty, you are already certainly, preternaturally tired. The road to where you are going is endless, nebulous, and painfully slow; you might not actually ever reach the destination in your lifetime.

We only see you in a Godlike sense, but I know you are also something all too human, all too recognizable. Maybe I am a dreamer. I know you had to have been one for a long time, before the dream became real and became something more like a snare. At your height, young man, you, quite arguably, will be (for a time) a more recognizable entity on this globe than Jesus Christ himself. How horrible. Did you ever even agree to this? Or was the next step just added to the constant to-do list that became your life—the life of the performer. The only way off the hamster wheel of success is suicide, I think, and quite arguably you did that too, but let's not let this get heavy for right now (we will get waaaaaaaaaay heavier later). I wish I could say we lived in a world that was much different for little Black boys these days— *progress not perfection*, they say—but some argue there's little of either. We are in danger still—more so every day; I hate that the powers that be said to you, "Here, little Black boy, go be sexy all the time," and you had to comply.

We still have to sing for our supper. The blue ribbons still go to those of us who can dance the best, sing the best, emote the best, but they say very little as to how much we are actually suffering. "I stifle my screams as frequently as I flash my smile; it means nothing," said a famous poet—and God, it's all too real. Our only safety is in danger, and performing as oneself for a murderous audience is certainly danger personified. I, like every other boy who wanted to be you, wanted to do the impossible: dance my way through gang violence (like in the "Beat It" video and "Bad"). We wanted to defy the laws of physics and moonwalk across the stage (your future self is going to do that at the 1983 Grammys—the magnetic poles of the earth shift that night) and also, just like your lyrics "oh, just leave me alone," sometimes we wanted to be left with our autonomy. This respect is not always granted to us. I think I'm supposed to say something here—about, like, I dunno, how many men are abused but they themselves don't turn into abusers. But oh God, I'm not quite sure how much I believe this. Furthermore, I, for one, am always keener to examine what the AVERAGE MEAN of people would do, not the exceptions to the rule.

But God, aren't you like the PEAK example of "exceptional"? The average person does ABOUT what one would expect; we do so love the examples of men who can walk in the rain and not get wet—you are only eleven. The letter I WANT to write you is probably for you at a later age, but the little boy in me can't write it yet. My heart still aches for all us little Black boys—I couldn't call you a monster or a god—I mean, if only, but I (unfortunately) don't have the power it takes to elevate or dismantle you; you occupy too much of the personified star/celebrity. But also, you do seem rooted in this kind of void that Heaven help me is so dark and perilous. I would be lying if I said I wasn't some form of fascinated enough to try and name it. But like I said, I can't call it. Furthermore, I can't call you at all—you at eleven are just as dead as you will be at fifty—the drug you took to ease the pain caused by the fact that you had been a ballerina since you were five; the wear and tear on your little body and little soul added to your death, but again, this is the future.

Me or anyone pretending to know anything about you is simply that: pretending. Many of us will never become living gods in our own lifetime, never deal with the demands of our personal autonomy being ripped from us before the age where we can fully consent (this is a KEY factor here, mind you!). It is one thing for some observer to say, "I simply don't understand"—that much I would allow—but for someone to say, "I don't understand how it got so out of control." They called you evil/freak/faggot from the time your voice refused to change and quite arguably before you could even conceive of the subject of sex (you are eleven currently, and people will still forgive you for sounding like a girl, but in the near future, the price you will pay for not dropping your register a few octaves is HORRIBLE). They will call you evil/freak/faggot so long that one day you will deliver it to them—is that how that works? Oh God, let me stop . . .

No. I know that if we live long enough, if we are lucky enough to see it, we will be, in turns, both gods and monsters; human casualties, sacrifices on an alter to pop culture. Oh, Michael, future father to present son, present son to dead father, Black boy to Black boy, "how it all got so out of control" is probably about the only thing I understand about it. But all I know is that you, at this present moment in the distant past, that you at eleven years old, most certainly deserve your flowers. Not that the rules of gravity EVER applied to someone like you. One day, you will float away.

Rest, Father.
Old man/Young man

Love,
Brontez

A RECIPE FOR HOME

BY CHEF RŌZE TRAORE

MOM,

I know you wanted me to be a doctor. Why else would you uproot yourself? Cross an ocean to the land of opportunity, then push farther to the far side of the continent, Seattle, a place as far-flung from your native Côte d'Ivoire as Mars. You braved shit weather and white faces and all that was unfamiliar. You set your eyes on a mission—build your business. A modest hair salon. I heard the bangs of hammer and nail and the *snip snip* of your thin scissors waft from our basement for months, then years, until you moved up and away, got a place of your own—then two—to house your hair kingdom, just like you said you would.

I know you wanted me to be a doctor.

Seattle had but one precious thing you recognized: the sea. Life in Côte d'Ivoire shaped itself around the coastline. Though it was a different ocean, you recognized the waves lapping Seattle's seaport as something like home. And maybe because he missed home, maybe because it was all he knew, maybe because he wanted me to be a doctor, Dad gave himself to that sea, left for months at a time on vessels bound for Alaska, chasing salmon and sea bass and whatever other treasures he could haul.

You did your part to bring the sea and, by extension, Côte d'Ivoire itself into our home. Many times a week, more than I care to remember, you fried tilapia the Ivorian way, adding your bright spices, and though I never knew home the way you did, I smelled it in the kitchen, saw it on the plate, felt it in my belly.

Côte d'Ivoire was never my home the way it was yours. You raised an American African. But soon, I wanted to put my home on a plate. So I left. Not for med school but for Paris. Then London. Then New York. Searching for wherever home was; carrying you with me.

I spent time in the most renowned kitchens in the world, learned French techniques; got good, then great. Refined what these European and American masters taught.

But it wasn't home. Not yet, at least. I had to blend what you showed me. I needed the sea.

"I didn't come all this way for you to cook, child." You wanted me to be a doctor. I made it a long way before you understood. But then you saw your baby on TV. You opened the *New York Times* and saw my face. You started to come around. Maybe one day your grandbabies can be doctors instead.

Sometimes you let me cook for you. Not often but sometimes. I try to show you what I've learned, how I've married your heritage with my experience. How I call on the sea.

You think it's aight.

To me, it's home.

Your son,
Rōze

HOME

Seared Chilean Sea Bass with Celery Root Puree and Golden Mushrooms

1 celery root	lemongrass	chives
1 white onion	bay leaf	parsley
1 Yukon potato	2 sprigs thyme	cracked pepper
grapeseed oil	1 sprig rosemary	1 lemon
salt	2 cloves garlic	3 oz sea bass
¼ cup white wine	1 stick of butter	canola oil
1 quart milk	1 bunch beech mushrooms	

Puree

- Trim and clean celery root, then cut into half-inch slices.
- Peel and julienne onion.

- Peel potato and cut into one-inch slices.
- Turn your heat on low to medium and drizzle enough grapeseed oil to coat the pan.
- Add the julienned onion, then season with a sprinkle of salt and let them sweat for about three minutes. Avoid color on your vegetables.
- Add wine and let the alcohol cook out for two minutes.
- Proceed by adding the potatoes and celery root to the pot, along with your milk.
- Season with salt; add lemongrass, bay leaf, and a sprig of thyme.
- Let this cook on low to medium heat for twenty-five to thirty minutes until your ingredients are tender and translucent.
- Once done, spoon out the onion, celery root, and potatoes, then add to a blender.
- Pour about one-fourth of a cup of the reserved liquid into the blender and turn it on high (avoid the lemongrass and thyme).
- While the blender is on, add one tsp butter and blend until all your ingredients are incorporated and smooth. Season to taste.
- Place it on the side to keep warm.

Mushrooms

- Split your mushrooms into individual pieces.
- Slice a chiffonade of chives and parsley.

- Preheat pan to medium heat.
- Drizzle enough grapeseed oil to coat the bottom of the pan, then add mushrooms and season with salt and cracked pepper.
- Cook for about five minutes or until golden brown.
- Turn your heat off and zest and squeeze a wedge of lemon into the mushrooms, followed by the chiffonade of chives and parsley.
- Place to the side to keep warm.

Fish

- Season fish with salt on both sides.
- Preheat your pan on low heat.
- Drizzle enough canola oil to coat the bottom of the pan.
- Place fish in the pan, skin-side down.
- Let fish cook for about four to five minutes or until the skin is golden.
- Once crispy, turn the fish flesh-side down and add one tbsp of butter, thyme, rosemary, and smashed garlic.
- Once butter is melted and partially foamy, turn the heat off.
- Baste it on top of the fish for two minutes.
- Remove the fish from the pan and begin plating.

SO I CAN FACE THE FEAR OF LIVING

BY SOJOURNER BROWN

Fret not thyself, I say.
Enough. You are plenty.

Your skin was beautiful, beautiful
skin. Your full lips, thick curls,
your cinnamon tangles
your terra-cotta curves
were some kind of
wonderful.

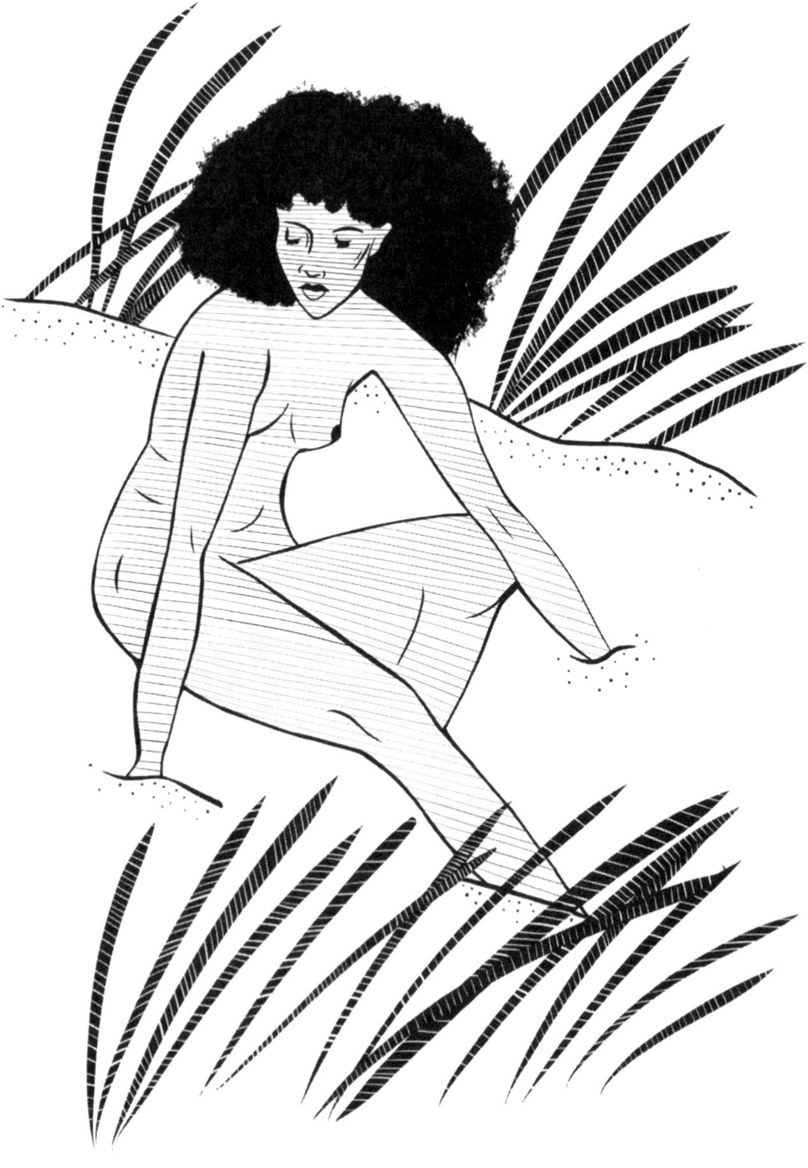

You were a masterpiece completed,
the astronomical line at the end of this obsidian
race. You were the footprint of the world
found in a pool of black glass,
a shimmering surface.
Your black was on purpose.
You were the sidewalk
sparkles, the ink left on
fingertips, the coffee cup rings on the
single blade of grass,
the concrete DNA, coded
light speed, in shades.

Strong like ovibos,
brave as raven,
free as a satellite
drifting through space.
A lone rover,
unbroken, for who could break you?
You thought you had seen the worst of your days.
You had wounds that cut deeper than any saber,
but your skin was renewed elastic, ablaze.

You were a comet, a slingshot,
the hydraulic cycle,
a diamond in the ash,

unearthed and remade.
You stood by the ocean,
dipped your toes in the dark,
you were loved by the senses,
you counted the waves.
Enough! You were enough.
You are more than enough.

Sojourner Brown

DEAR INNER CRITIC

BY JENNA WORTHAM

Thank you. Thank you for all that you have done to protect me from being harmed in the world. It took me a while to recognize you; even longer to understand that, though your words ring loudly in my head, they are not the truth. I'm sorry it took me so long to truly see that you were not conspiring for me to fail but doing your best to help me succeed. We made you together, to weather a harsh environment, to navigate an environment and a culture that inherently devalues us.

Your words no longer keep me safe; they now actively stand in the way of my growth. I no longer draw power from being the first to point out my mistakes, momentary shortcomings, bouts of forgetfulness. I am no longer under the illusion that it is productive to tear myself down, that it keeps me from making mistakes in the future.

Compassion is my new compass. I no longer need to blame, shame, judge, or gossip about other people to make myself feel better. I no longer need to cut others down to lift myself up. I no longer need to punish myself. I am worthy of love; I am worthy of my life. I am doing my best, and it is enough. I make mistakes, and I am human. I am able to forgive myself—and you. Thank you for everything. Your work here is done.

Yours, J

DEAR WATER

BY JAN MENAFEE

I came to you once, ready to die.

But as I stood on the banks of your river,
I heard your singing for what felt like the first time.
I followed your flow until the bend,
And wondered where you were headed.

Something about you reminded me
of my grandmother and how I wished
I remembered more about her.
Yet somewhere in my encounter with you,
I felt her presence giving me strength.

It was as if you were one spirit and body of water,
Reminding me that whatever pain I felt would pass.
You assured me that it was okay to feel afraid.
That fear doesn't last forever,

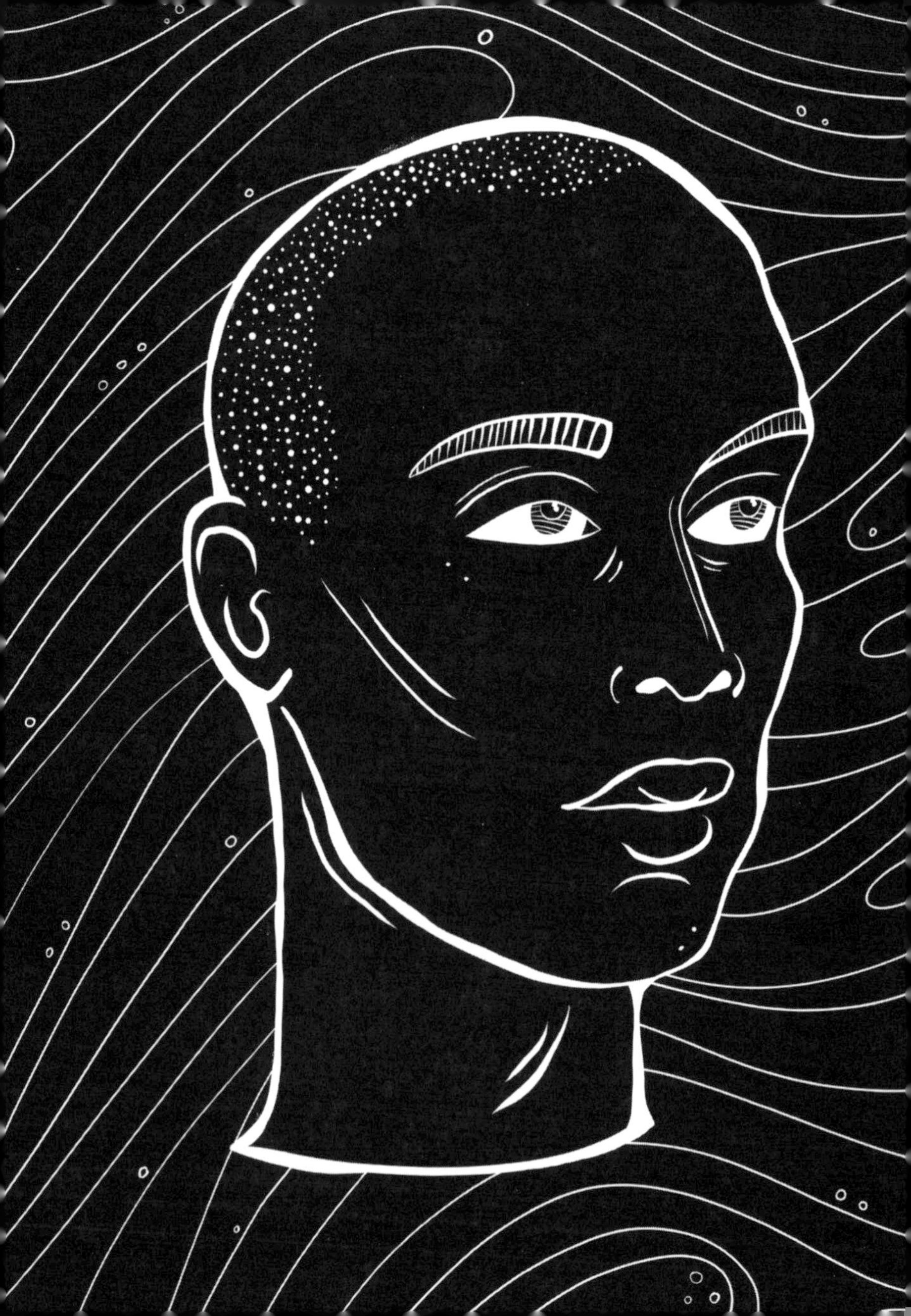

But the love we have for each other does,
Even in death.

As I grow up in an uncertain world,
Where they have poisoned and polluted our bodies,
I wonder how we will ever heal.

How can we love and be loved
Given all the pain we've endured at their hands
And our own?

You never stop giving life to me and all my loved ones,
Though we take life from you.
Certain structures, not of our making, are invested
In our forgetting and neglecting our bodies of water
Because we are easier to divide and conquer that way.

Our power to resist, abolish, and transform
The world lies deep within us
And through your many forms.
All we have to do is return to you.

I read, listen, and learn all I can,
And all of my reaching for an answer
Just brings me back to my childhood.

Many of my most vivid memories are ones
Where I felt most alive.
And I have always felt most alive with you:
Under your clouds,
At your shores,
In your rivers,
Lakes,
Oceans,
And in my most intimate moments
Cooking with my mother in our kitchen,
Cleansing myself in our bathroom.

There was a time when I knew love,
Wholeness and connection with you
And the world around me.
I could spend hours and hours in your embrace—
No matter what form you took.

What happened to that kid who loved you,
Water, with all his heart?

After years of feeling lost, hurt, and betrayed,
I returned to you.
I used to take you for granted,
but since that day that I came to you ready to die,

I take you as my grandmother.
My greatest teacher
Who's never said a word
Because you don't need to.

You've taught me how special and sacred
Our lives are as Black bodies of water.

You've taught me that as far as
I might feel from you, myself,
Or the family I've known and will never know,
I can remember that we're all right here,
Closer than ever.

You've taught me to have faith
Because those who take care of us
Cannot always be seen
But should be praised nonetheless.

I'm starting to believe that you love us
In many ways, both mysterious and mundane.
But you'll never say I love you with words.
No words will ever fully contain
The love, wonder, gratitude, respect,
Fear, anger, shame, and doubt

That I have ever felt for you either.
Let alone those feelings for you from all of us.

Because even though we often call you a resource,
You're more like a relative:
At once our oldest ancestor
And our youngest descendant.

TO FAMILY, ALPHABET MAFIA, TISH 'N' NEM, JAYSON NEM, LANGSTON NEM, AND MAYBE YOU

BY DANEZ SMITH

When we were small, we loved ourselves and were told we got it wrong, that we loved the wrong person. Some of us borrowed the eyes of others to hate our reflections, some of us were kicked out of our homes for refusing to take on the role of someone else, some of us buried ourselves deep into the dirt thrown at our true names, unable to dig ourselves up until years later, some of us go to the grave already in the grave. In your face, they said you don't exist. Or you were encouraged, your mama got it even if your granny and aunties didn't, you walked out into the world, and that's when you learned the casualness of cruelty (though you've been cruel to others, to yourself).

Cruelty. All over who you love, the fact that you love. All over who you are, the fact that you are. All because you have a body and refuse to hate it, because you don't limit yourself for people who have loved and created and feared the boundaries they police at you. Or you limited yourself; you cut corners off yourself until you were vague even to yourself, and it took years, is taking years, to arrive at a version of yourself that you keep or kept illegal and at a distance for the sake of someone else or for housing or for family or for safety.

Black, possible, queer child. Black beautiful stud. Black alluring sissy. Black unbounded them. Black bold man. Black incredible woman. Wherever you are in your journey along yourself, whether out or still sheltered from view, young or old, new or studied in this knowing of yourself, you are loved. You deserve a better world than the one offered to you. But, for years, we have found this second family of ours in smoky rooms and songs, in poems and down at the bar, in secret circles at church, in glances and the theater and the bookstore, and in exes and apps and the ball and gym and the backseat and the Navy and class and the corner and shelter and job corps and the bus and giveaway and bowling alley and barbershop and under braiding hands and with somebody's cousin and all the ways blood or otherwise we make family happen. My mafia, my quilt. I pray love and every good year into your life. May your pleasure be God's delight. May you find yourself in rooms where your laugh is big and honest. May the world that hates you know a quick poison. May your tomorrow bloom long. Our rise to our life is no crystal stair, but we keep making it there. I am so proud of all y'all. What someone once tried to make me feel was an affliction has not just been my nature but, at times, my treasure. One of the ways I tied me to you, a golden thread next to the one of bright onyx.

I love you right as you are.

Danez

MY BLACK BODY

BY MALACHI ELIJAH

My Black body has been loved. Has it been cherished? My Black body's been kissed. Has it been held? My Black body's been touched. Has it been felt? My Black body is resented. My Black body is wanted. Once upon a time, my Black body was needed. And still. It is. My Black body is of the Earth. Look at how we treat our

Earth.

My Black body is a storm. There's calm, and there's destruction. All trapped in here. Wind gashes it. The breeze possesses it. My Black body is like water, at once clear and fresh; we fight its pollution more than we nurture its body. MY! Black! Body! is a flower. Let it blossom. My Black body is pollen sprinkled on a bee. My Black body is a seed dispersed by a sneeze-like gust. My Black body is not the tree but the fruit. Strange. My Black body is honest. Any falsehood you, we, or I hold is not our own. These Black bodies are constantly undoing something taught by fools who dig only as deep as they are paid to, want to, think to, prey to. Strong, assertive, vulnerable, pure is my Black body. Not stained by disdain coming from a phobic mind frame. My Black body is a book you cannot skim through. My Black body is thoughtful. My Black body is curiously thirsting for knowledge of self.

Taught to be considerate. My Black body will make mistakes. My mind has not always recognized our bodies' beauty. My Black body is a temple. I should pray more often, meditate on that, and work it out, not drink, not drug. . . . But, *thinks of a clever line about how they do anyway. Deletes it for being contrived.*

My Black body is a gift.

Not a token or a prize. A cup, half full. My Black body is a mirror. What do you see? Some leave with a crack, while others reflect clearly. My Black body is music. Turn me on and dance with no care for who scoffs or stares. My Black body is quiet. My Black body is a deep breath, felt in the belly.

My Black body is a target for bullets and slurs. It's a good thing I pay no attention to your words. But the bullets? Well, it's not impenetrable, my Black body. It cuts, bruises, bleeds, and swells. You've put my Black body through hell for fear of the idea my

Black body is heavenly, earthly, and, firstly, divine. *Your being is too much for some people.* Some will feel there are too many "Black bodies" in this writing and may find it repetitive.

You are confused by my Black body. You could only hope to understand. Until that day, mock, murder, mimic, maim. My. Black. Body. My Black body is ash, so I moisturize daily. Soaking in cocoa and shea mixed with only the sun.

This Black body is one of one.

Stunning.

My Black body is present and restless. My Black body has already been buried. My Black body is alive. Until it isn't.

ACKNOWLEDGMENTS

We want to thank the contributors, who've trusted us with their stories, their truths, and their vulnerability. This idea was a seed when we approached many of you. Your words not only inspired every piece of art contained in these pages but also brought the book to life.

To Mike Jackson and John Legend—thank you for taking a chance on this project. This could not have happened without you. To Emily Bell, Caolinn Douglas, Molly Stern, and the team at Zando—thank you for all the love you poured into this work. You have been the caretakers of our dream, and we are eternally grateful.

To Abby Walters and Jamie Stockton—thank you for believing in our work, having our backs, and keeping our best interests always at heart.

To our families and our closest friends—thank you for being the sounding boards for many crazy ideas brought forth over the last two years. But most of all, thank you for the sustenance that allowed us to carry this project from beginning to end.

Finally, to bell hooks, whose seminal book *All About Love* was the kernel for this project—you taught us that love is an action: love is as love does. We hope we've done just that.

CREDITS AND PERMISSIONS

CONTRIBUTORS

AKILI KING is a journalist and senior editor at Rose Inc. During her time as a beauty editor at *Vogue*, she created a column, "Texture Diaries," that celebrates and affirms Black beauty, which she still writes to this day. Additionally, King writes for various magazines—where her writing spans topics such as beauty, wellness, culture, and music—including the Cut's "Auto-Refill" column, *Essence*, Coveteur, *Allure*, and many others.

REVEREND AL SHARPTON is a renowned American civil rights activist, Baptist minister, politician, and host of the show *PoliticsNation* on MSNBC. Reverend Sharpton's lifelong pursuit of justice and equality began at the age of four when he preached his first sermon. Sharpton is the founder of the National Action Network, one of the leading civil rights organizations in the world.

ALEXANDRA ELLE is a wellness educator and author of the *New York Times* bestseller *How We Heal: Uncover Your Power and Set Yourself Free*. She dedicates her work to building community and healing practices through literature and language. Elle teaches workshops and courses to help others find their voices and create clarity in their lives and relationships.

ALLISA CHARLES-FINDLEY is president of the Botham Jean Foundation, which was created after her twenty-six-year-old brother, Botham Jean, was murdered by an off-duty police officer in his apartment in Dallas, Texas. His name became a rallying cry for nationwide protests, and Findley has since worked to keep his name alive by promoting Christian intervention for social change, justice for police brutality victims, and police reform.

BARBARA EDELIN is an activist for reproductive justice and the President of B. Edelin Events Planning, which she runs with her daughter, Corinne. Edelin is the wife of the late Dr. Kenneth Edelin, the pioneering physician known for his support of abortion rights and advocacy for the disadvantaged. In 1975, Dr. Edelin gained national attention after he was convicted for performing a legal abortion by an all-white, predominantly Catholic jury. The conviction was later overturned by the Massachusetts Supreme Court, serving as a landmark trial of civil and reproductive rights.

BELINDA WALKER is a senior TV producer at MSNBC and a playwright who believes that every story can find an audience when told with ingenuity, heart, and style.

BEN CRUMP is a civil rights and personal injury attorney who has dedicated his legal career to fighting discrimination and the pursuit of justice for victims of police violence. Referred to as "Black America's Attorney General," he is the recipient of the NAACP Social Justice Impact Award and listed among the Most Influential People of 2021 by

TIME 100 and *Ebony* magazine's Power 100 Most Influential African Americans.

BILL WHITAKER is a television journalist who has covered major news stories for over four decades. In 2014, he became a correspondent for CBS News's *60 Minutes*, which has taken him to Asia, Africa, Europe, Mexico, and the Middle East. Whitaker is the 2018 winner of the Radio Television Digital News Association's highest honor, the Paul White Award for career achievement, and has won numerous other awards, including a Peabody and two duPont-Columbia Awards.

BILQUISU ABDULLAH is a student in Washington, DC, studying women's and gender studies and medical humanities. She loves all things reading, writing, and grounding. If she's not in class, you can most likely find her on a rooftop listening to music. The person who has inspired her most in life to celebrate love is her Nana. She continues to discover love through chats with her mom, time spent with her siblings, and traveling.

BRIANNA HOLT is a journalist and screenwriter. She is also the author of *In Our Shoes: On Being a Young Black Woman in Not-So "Post-Racial" America*, a debut essay collection that dissects and analyzes stereotypes that millennial Black women are expected to live up to.

BRONTEZ PURNELL is a multi-hyphenate artist and writer. He is the author of several books, including *Since I Laid My Burden Down*, which received the 2018 Whiting Award in Fiction. He is also the editor of the zine *Fag School* and serves as the front man of the punk band The Younger Lovers. Purnell's films have been showcased at the Berkeley Art Museum, Visual Aids in New York, and The Lab in San Francisco. Purnell's explorations of dance, writing, and film emphasize a radically open understanding of form and body, creating work that marries punk-rock subversion and free jazz improvisation.

DANEZ SMITH is a poet, writer, and performer. They are the author of three poetry collections, including *Homie* and *Don't Call Us Dead*, which have won the Forward Prize for Best Collection, the Minnesota Book Award in Poetry, and the Lambda Literary Award for Gay Poetry. Their works have also been finalists for the NAACP Image Award in Poetry, the National Book Critic Circle Award, and the National Book Award. Smith has also been featured as part of *Forbes*'s annual 30 Under 30 list and is the winner of a Pushcart Prize. They live in Minnesota near their people.

DICK PARSONS is an American business executive who served as the chairman of Citigroup and chairman and CEO of Time Warner. Parsons's civic and nonprofit commitments include chairman of the Jazz Foundation of America, co-chairman of the Mayor's Commission on Economic Opportunity in New York, chairman emeritus of the Partnership for New York City, chairman of the Apollo Theater Foundation, and service on the boards of The National Museum of African American History and Culture and Teach for America.

DEBORAH WILLIS is a pioneering artist, author, and curator. Her innovative art and research has focused on cultural histories envisioning the Black body, women, and gender. Willis is a celebrated photographer, acclaimed historian of photography, MacArthur and Guggenheim Fellow, and university professor and chair of the Department of Photography & Imaging at the Tisch School of the Arts at New York University. She is the recipient of two NAACP Image Awards for her co-authored book *Envisioning Emancipation* (with Barbara Krauthamer) and for the documentary *Through a Lens Darkly*, inspired by her book *Reflections in Black: A History of Black Photographers, 1840 to the Present*.

DOUG JONES is the author of the debut novel *Prime Real Estate*, a story set in the 1996 Olympics of two Black men confronting their roles in displacing Black residents to make way for the opening ceremony while coming to terms with their sexuality. Jones is a Columbia MFA alum and Lambda Literary inaugural fellow.

DOUGLAS KEARNEY is a poet, performer, and librettist. He is the author of seven books, including *Sho*, which was a finalist for the National Book Award, PEN America Literary Award, and Minnesota Book Award. He has also received a Whiting Writer's Award, a Foundation for Contemporary Arts Cy Twombly Award for Poetry, as well as residencies and fellowships from Cave Canem, The Rauschenberg Foundation, and others. Kearney is a professor of creative writing at the University of Minnesota–Twin Cities, where he is a McKnight Presidential Fellow.

IMANI PERRY is the Hughes-Rogers Professor of African American Studies at Princeton University and a columnist for the *Atlantic*. She is the author of seven books, including the *New York Times* bestselling *South to America: A Journey Below the Mason-Dixon to Understand the Soul of a Nation*, which received the 2022 National Book Award for nonfiction, and the multi-award winning titles *May We Forever Stand: A History of the Black National Anthem* and *Looking for Lorraine: The Radiant and Radical Life of Lorraine Hansberry*.

JAMILA WOODS is an award-winning poet and musician born and raised on the South Side of Chicago. Her work blurs the boundaries between poem and song to create rich sonic worlds that fuse personal and historical narratives. She has released two critically acclaimed studio albums, *Heavn* (2017) and *Legacy! Legacy!* (2019). Her third album is forthcoming in October 2023, and she is currently working on her debut book of poems.

JAN MENAFEE is a poet, podcaster, and educational designer based in Chicago, Illinois, and Washington, DC. He loves to create and collaborate in the waters of Black culture, ecology, and community building.

JAYNE ALLEN is a writer, producer, entrepreneur, and forever recovering lawyer. Purposeful in centering and celebrating Black women's societal contributions, Allen crafts transcultural stories that explore contemporary issues such as modern relationships, workplace and career dynamics, fertility, and the complexities of race. Her common themes include mental and physical health awareness and highlight the importance of self-love and self-care. Allen is the author of the bestselling Black Girls Must Die Exhausted trilogy and is working on her first stand-alone novel.

JEH CHARLES JOHNSON is an American lawyer and former government official. He served as secretary of homeland security and general counsel of the Defense Department under President Obama. A decorated statesman, Johnson's proudest achievement is co-authoring the report that paved the way for the repeal of the "Don't Ask, Don't Tell" policy by Congress, allowing LGBTQ service members to serve openly in the US military. He is the recipient of twelve honorary degrees and a graduate of Morehouse College, class of 1979.

JENNA WORTHAM is a staff writer for the *New York Times Magazine* and co-host of the *NYT* podcast *Still Processing*. They are the co-editor of the visual anthology *Black Futures*, a 2020 Editors' Choice by the *New York Times Book Review*. Wortham is a sound healer, reiki practitioner, herbalist, and community care worker who is oriented toward healing, justice, and liberation. They are also currently working on a book about the body and dissociation called *Work of Body*.

JONATHAN CAPEHART is a Pulitzer Prize–winning journalist and political commentator. He is an associate editor of the *Washington Post*, a contributor to *Brooks and Capehart* on PBS NewsHour, and the host of *The Saturday Show* and *The Sunday Show* on MSNBC. In 2022, the National LGBTQ Task Force presented Capehart with the National Leadership Award for advancing freedom, justice, and full equality for LGBTQ Americans.

JOEL CASTÓN is a formerly incarcerated Washingtonian who serves as a mentor, author, and activist for criminal justice reform. He is one of the founding mentors of the Young Men Emerging Unit at the DC

Jail, a program designed to empower recently incarcerated people and change the culture of corrections through youth mentorship, job training, and educational programming. In June 2021, Castón made history when he was elected as an advisory neighborhood commissioner (ANC), becoming the first incarcerated person to hold public office in Washington, DC.

JOY-ANN REID is an award-winning cable news host and political analyst for MSNBC. She is the author of the *New York Times* bestseller *The Man Who Sold America: Trump and the Unraveling of the American Story*, as well as *Fracture: Barack Obama, the Clintons, and the Racial Divide* and *We Are the Change We Seek: The Speeches of Barack Obama*. Her show, *The ReidOut*, interviews politicians and newsmakers, and focuses on race, justice, and culture.

JUSTUS CORNELIUS PUGH is a South Side Chicago–bred storyteller, poet, and technologist. Pugh is creator and steward of "Afrotranscendental"—a school of thought, dream archive, and experience lab that explores Black culture, spirituality, and ancestry.

KWAME DAWES is the author of numerous books of poetry and other books of fiction, criticism, and essays. His most recent collection, *unHistory*, was co-written with John Kinsella. Dawes is a George W. Holmes University Professor of English and Glenna Luschei Editor of *Prairie Schooner*. He teaches in the Pacific MFA Program and is the series editor of the African Poetry Book Series, director of the African Poetry Book Fund, and artistic director of the Calabash International Literary Festival. He is a chancellor for the Academy of American Poets and a fellow of the Royal Society of Literature. Dawes is the winner of the prestigious Windham/Campbell Prize for Poetry and was a finalist for the 2022 Neustadt International Prize for Literature. In 2022 Dawes was awarded the Order of Distinction Commander class by the government of Jamaica.

LYNAE VANEE BOGUES is an NAACP Image Award–nominated performer, poet, influencer, writer, and actress. She uses her digital platforms to speak on race, feminism, politics, and inclusivity, and her viral videos have garnered over twenty million views and the attention of several celebrities, major networks, and the general public.

MAHOGANY BROWNE is a writer, playwright, organizer, and educator. In 2022, she was selected as one of the Kennedy Center's Next 50 leaders and a Wesleyan University Distinguished Writer-in-Residence. Browne serves as the executive director of JustMedia and the artistic director of Urban Word. She has authored several works, including *Vinyl Moon, Chlorine Sky, Woke: A Young Poet's Call to Justice, Woke Baby,* and *Black Girl Magic.* Founder of the diverse lit initiative Woke Baby Book Fair, Browne's latest poetry collection is *Chrome Valley.* She is the first-ever poet-in-residence at the Lincoln Center and lives in Brooklyn, New York.

MALACHI ELIJAH is a musician, performer, songwriter, and part of the hip-hop collective SPACE CADE7S. Elijah also works in providing mentorship and artistic development for historically marginalized teens and young adults with the nonprofit Art Start in New York City.

MICHAEL ERIC DYSON is a distinguished professor, media personality, and author of multiple *New York Times* bestsellers, including *Tears We Cannot Stop*, *What Truth Sounds Like*, *JAY-Z*, and *Long Time Coming*. A winner of the 2018 nonfiction Southern Book Prize, Dr. Dyson is also a recipient of two NAACP Image awards and the 2020 Langston Hughes Festival Medallion. Former president Barack Obama has noted: "Everybody who speaks after Michael Eric Dyson pales in comparison." He serves as University Distinguished Professor of African American and Diaspora Studies of Ethics and Society and NEH Centennial Chair at Vanderbilt University.

MORGAN JERKINS is a writer and editor based in Harlem. She is the author of the *New York Times* bestseller *This Will Be My Undoing* as well as the critically acclaimed books *Wandering in Strange Lands* and *Caul Baby*. A *Forbes* 30 Under 30 Leader in Media alumna and ASME Next award-winning journalist, Jerkins has been an editor at *Medium*, *ESPN*, and *New York* magazine, among others. She's held professorships at Pacific University, Leipzig University in Germany, Columbia University, and the New School.

NADIA OWUSU is a writer and memoirist. Her debut book *Aftershocks* received a 2019 Whiting Award for nonfiction and was selected as a best book of 2021 by *TIME*, *Vogue*, *Esquire*, the *Guardian*, NPR, the BBC, and others. It was one of President Barack Obama's favorite books of the year, a *New York Times Book Review* Editors' Choice, and a 2021 Goodreads Choice Award nominee. It was also chosen by Nobel Peace Prize laureate Malala Yousafzai for her Literati book club.

RAKIA REYNOLDS is a thought leader, tastemaker, and branding expert who advises name brands on creative strategy. She serves as founder and executive officer of Skai Blue Media, a nontraditional communications agency that proudly hosts an eclectic group of storytellers, brand experts, and strategists. With a guiding principle of distilling equity in messaging, Reynolds has been named by *Inc.* magazine as one of the 27 Business Leaders Aiming to Change the World. She was also listed as one of the 25 Most Socially Influential Tastemakers on Dell's "Inspire 100" list and profiled by *Forbes* on their "Next 1000" list.

RHIANNA JONES is a writer, activist, and model. Her passions are sustainable fashion, female narratives, and cultural inclusivity, and her viral Afro Emoji campaign started a global convo about beauty norms.

CHEF RŌZE TRAORE is a chef, media personality, and entrepreneur. He is the creator of unique dining experiences for clients and brands such as the *New York Times*, Veuve Clicquot, Dior, and Louis Vuitton. Throughout his career, Traore has made it his mission to help those of every socioeconomic background, working to bring the pleasures of eating fresh, beautiful food to communities facing food insecurity.

SOJOURNER BROWN is a poet and multidisciplinary artist based in Brooklyn, New York. Her writing has been published in literary journals, and she has been a featured guest in spoken-word events at the Nuyorican Poets Cafe and other venues across NYC. Additionally, as an artist, Brown is currently in the cast of *Hadestown* on Broadway, and her work as an actor and vocalist has been seen on Disney Channel,

Freeform, NBC, and at Carnegie Hall. She is currently working on an upcoming EP and a poetry book debut.

TARANA BURKE has been an activist, advocate, and author for more than twenty-five years, working at the intersection of sexual violence and racial justice. Fueled by commitments to interrupt sexual violence and other systemic inequalities disproportionately impacting marginalized people, particularly Black women and girls, Burke has created and led various campaigns focused on increasing access to resources and supporting impacted communities, including the "me too." Movement, which has galvanized millions of survivors and allies around the world, and the "me too." international nonprofit organization, founded in 2018. Her *New York Times* bestselling books *You Are Your Best Thing* and *Unbound* have illuminated the power of healing, vulnerability, and storytelling in the movement to end sexual violence.

TEMBE DENTON-HURST is a writer at *New York* magazine who focuses on beauty, books, and culture. She is also the author of the debut novel *Homebodies*, a story of losing yourself and finding the road back home.

TOPAZ JONES is a rapper, singer, and producer from Montclair, New Jersey. In 2021, he released the album *Don't Go Tellin' Your Momma* and directed a short film to accompany the album of the same name, which won the Sundance Film Festival Short Film Jury Award and South by Southwest's Special Jury Recognition for Visionary Storytelling.

TRACEY MICHAE'L LEWIS-GIGGETTS is a writer, thought leader, and the author or collaborator of twenty books in several genres. She is the host of the podcast *HeARTtalk with Tracey Michae'l*, and founder of HeARTspace, a healing community created to serve those who have experienced trauma of any kind through the use of storytelling and the arts. Lewis-Giggetts's book, *Black Joy: Stories of Resistance, Resilience, and Restoration*, won the 2023 NAACP Image Award for Outstanding Literary Work-Instructional.

VJ JENKINS is a poet, writer, and civil rights attorney at the Department of Justice. As an attorney, Jenkins works to ensure that all people feel safe, seen, heard, and valued in the workplace by targeting institutions that perpetuate discriminatory workplace policies. As a poet-writer, VJ uses his work as a mechanism to explore self—Blackness and queerness are his leading muses. His greatest hope is that his writing inspires an ethos in every Black child that they deserve more love than the world says they do.

ABOUT THE EDITORS

COLE BROWN is an author, producer, and political commentator. His first book, *Greyboy: Finding Blackness in a White World*, was a finalist for an NAACP Image Award and selected for Stephen Curry's Underrated book club. His first coauthored book, *First Impressions*, was released in May 2022. Cole's opinion writing appears in *GQ*, *W*, and on CNN.com, NBC.com, and others. He was a 2022 *Forbes* 30 Under 30 Honoree in Media. Today, he lives in New York working on various literary and film projects.

NATALIE JOHNSON is a writer and illustrator who focuses on racial justice and gender equality. As an artist, she mixes digital and traditional media. She creates illustrations that combine sharp, high-contrast designs with a feeling of softness and vulnerability. She is also a former segment producer for MSNBC, Vice TV, and Black News Channel. Her various writings can be found at MSNBC.com's "Know Your Value." Natalie holds a master's degree in sociology from Columbia University, where she studied gender, sexuality, and economic sociology.

Namesake

For
Joycetta

My
Black
Body

A recipe for home

Dear
Mom

Dear Black
america

Dear Uncle micki

To self